Profit from
Dynamic People Management

PICSIE BOOKS
P.O. Box 786340
Sandton 2146
Tel (011) 442-8175

JOHN HUMPHREY
&
BRIAN ANGUS

Profit from Dynamic People Management

JUTA & CO, LTD

CAPE TOWN • WETTON • JOHANNESBURG

First published in 1989

© Juta & Co, Ltd 1989
PO Box 14373, Kenwyn 7790

ISBN 0 7021 2293 9

Printed and bound in the Republic of South Africa by
Chelsea Press, Hillstar Avenue, Wetton

Contents

Introduction

Like most areas of specialised study, personnel management has developed its fair share of buzz words and jargon. If you want to study the subject in detail there are at least a hundred thick books you can read covering every aspect. Unfortunately the practical applications of all this wisdom are often not very clear and the contradictory views of the various experts can sometimes be downright confusing.

So for most managers, studying the science of people management is not a popular way of spending Saturday afternoon. Which is a pity when you consider that, in most organisations, the payroll represents somewhere between 30 and 50 % of their total costs.

Quite apart from the basic costs of employing people there are all the other costs involved in having to accommodate and equip them, which could add another 10–20 % on top, so that people-related costs are a major input in any business.

But what about the output from these people?

Business organisations depend wholly on the ability of their employees to produce more value than they consume in costs — to add value during the process which will enable the organisation to operate at a profit.

In the diagram on the next page, in case A the employees have boosted the value of the output by adding value during the process. In case B they have added nothing so that the value of the output

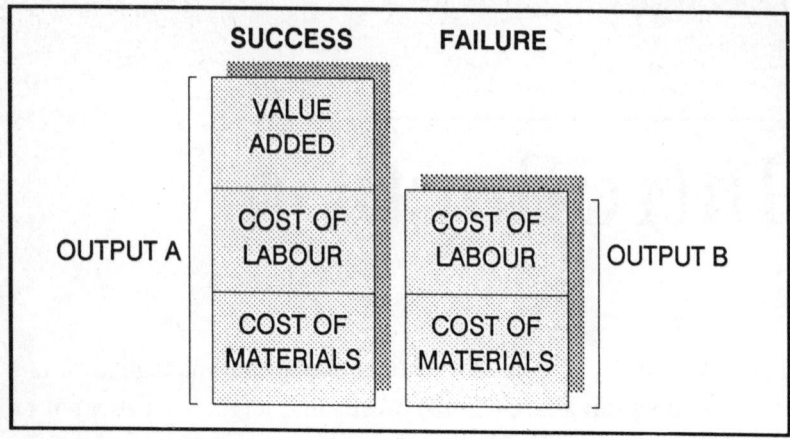

is only equal to the input costs. Added value is a major factor in determining profit, which is the name of the game in a free-market society such as the one in which we live.

Success in making a profit from people management doesn't just happen. It demands the application of management techniques and expertise by everyone responsible for the input and output of the human resources of an enterprise, from the most junior supervisor to the managing director.

A production manager wouldn't leave important policy decisions affecting his other resources — materials, machinery, facilities, etc — to outside agencies. Nor should he do so in the case of his most vital resource — manpower. Even if he is lucky enough to have the assistance of a personnel specialist he will be better able to appreciate and apply specialist advice if he himself has a clear understanding of how best to manage people.

So this little book is aimed at those managers and supervisors who want to learn, not only routine people management skills, but also, more importantly, how to implement dynamic (moving) as opposed to static (stationary) human resources management to the ultimate benefit of their employees, their organisations, and themselves.

1

People produce profit

Business organisations cannot survive without profit. Profit pays for expansion, development, and better wages and conditions for the people involved. Without profit businesses die.

This has always been a fact of business life but it is only comparatively recently that the vital role which *people* play in producing organisational profit has become fully realised by both managers and writers in the management field.

The reasons for this growing realisation of the importance of the people resource—at least in South Africa—are not difficult to find. Statistics in recent years on the so-called 'brain drain' indicate an alarming number of skilled people leaving the country to seek opportunities elsewhere. Consequently, competition between organisations to attract and hold on to good people has become more intense. To add to the problem, high levels of inflation in recent years have also put pressure on salary levels at a time when many organisations have been faced with reduced profitability. Employees at the lower levels in an organisation are no longer a cheap resource, and the rapid development of unions, particularly amongst lower-skilled workers, continues to put pressure on wages at these levels.

The result of these developments has been a rapid rise in staffing costs, which has forced organisations to pay closer attention to employment levels and to question the contribution of every single employee to the organisation's objectives.

Many researchers have now reached the conclusion that the real difference between successful organisations and their less successful (or unsuccessful) competitors is very often the way in which they manage their people. Unless the organisation's people resources are managed effectively, efforts to improve profits by attempting to produce better products, by implementing new marketing strategies or by instituting management controls are unlikely to succeed.

So today we are being forced to adopt a more sophisticated approach to people management. No longer can we adopt the old simplistic view that people merely have to be given a job and be paid fairly for doing it. This has been replaced by the realisation that organisations need to view their human resources from the same long-term perspective as they do their financial and physical resources.

This means that they must forecast not only how many people they will require in the medium to long term, but also precisely what skills they will need and how much they will have to pay for those skills (if indeed those skills are available). And, most importantly, organisations must do what they can to ensure that these people, once hired, will be fully productive.

Hence more and more organisations have begun to draw up training and development programmes for their employees. Formal manpower plans, once scarcer than hens' teeth, have become commonplace, even in smaller organisations. Human resource accounting systems have been introduced in an attempt to measure more accurately the costs of, and the contribution from, the organisation's people.

The general manager stared unhappily at the MD's remarks pencilled on his division's results report for the month. Although he felt the MD's criticism a bit harsh, there was little doubt that he was right — the problems did appear to lie mainly in his high operating costs, particularly those relating to staff. He suspected that parts of his operation were overstaffed, certainly if the amount of chatting and time wasting which seemed to go on in the various offices was anything to go by. He wasn't too happy about the general morale either. There had been a good deal of grumbling about the recent salary increases, although these had been as high as the company could afford at present levels of production.

On his desk lay a pamphlet from a firm offering various training courses for his staff. Would these solve the problem? An article he had read recently said that people were an organisation's most valuable asset. Maybe they were, but one thing was certain — they were by far its most expensive and problematic one.

The GM had finally realised that he had to begin looking more closely at his people resources. But where should he start? Human beings are, after all, very complex creatures.

There are many equally complex theories on how people should be managed. Despite this, there are some basic factors which we know affect human behaviour in the work situation. One of them is *motivation*.

After many years of argument on the relative merits of various theories of behaviour in the work situation the overwhelming weight of evidence now indicates that staff motivation is an absolutely vital factor in determining the success or failure of an organisation.

Motivation can be simply defined, in a business context, as *the drive or desire to exert effort*. When the drive is absent or of low intensity the worker will exert little effort. When it is high in intensity he will exert his maximum effort—he becomes *motivated*. So, in

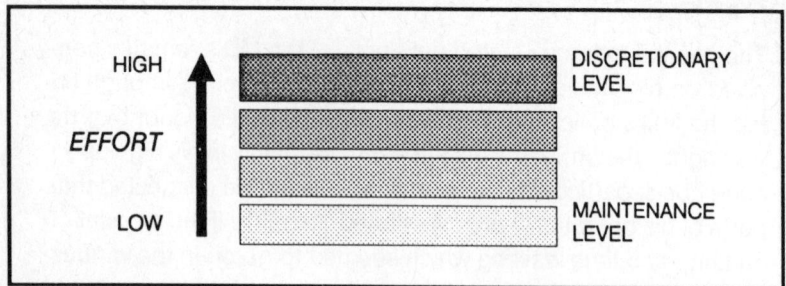

the work context, motivation relates essentially to the amount of effort which an individual is prepared to put into the job.

In a given work situation, will he exert only the minimum effort—which is known as the *maintenance* level of effort—required to get by without being punished or penalised? Will he meet just the minimum standards of performance? Or will he strive to do the job really well, and expend the extra effort—known as the *discretionary* level of effort—needed to do so? Or will he try for somewhere in between the most and the least?[*]

We have all encountered cases where employees opt for producing at a lower level than they could comfortably manage.

The important difference between these two types of effort is that whereas people can, generally speaking, be made or forced to perform to the minimum standards required, discretionary effort by its very nature is voluntary. It is very difficult, if not impossible, to force people to perform really well—they must want to do so. The adage says 'You can lead a horse to water but you can't make him drink.' To which we can add: 'But you can make him very thirsty!'

It is discretionary effort which differentiates the motivated from the unmotivated employee. It can also make a great contribution to the performance of an organisation—and its profits.

[*]The authors are indebted to Mr Norman McNally for the notion of maintenance and discretionary levels of effort.

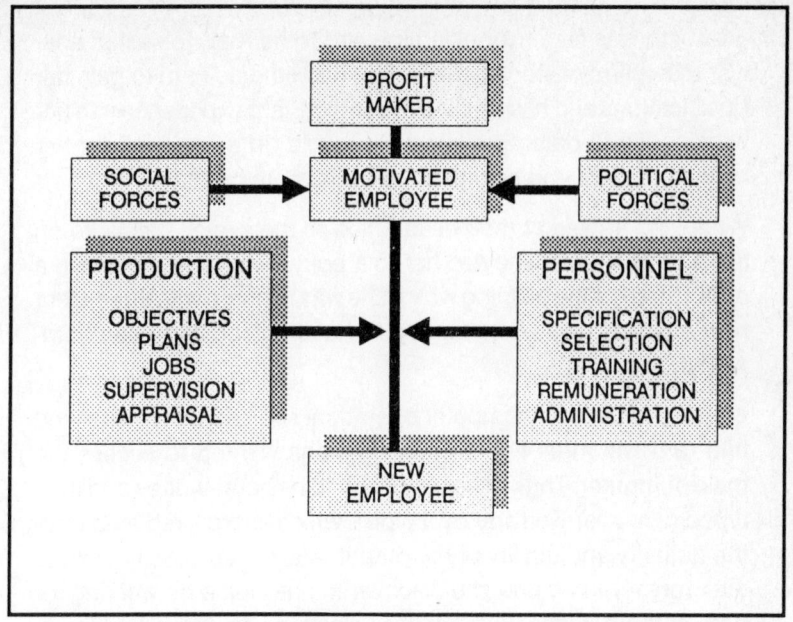

Usually when an employee first joins a company he is highly motivated and anxious to demonstrate his ability and desire to apply his discretionary effort to the job he has won for himself in the face of competition. He then comes into contact with the various systems, procedures and people of the organisation, all of which will influence him in one way or another. If their influence is positive he will remain a motivated employee able to deal with any negative social and political forces to which he may be exposed. Motivated employees are potential profit makers for the organisation.

On the other hand, if these factors prove to be a negative influence or if some of the essential ingredients are simply missing, he will rapidly lose any desire to apply anything more than the minimum maintenance effort necessary to stay in his job, and he will save his discretionary effort for more exciting things—such as his weekend fishing, rugby, or trade union activities.

Elizabeth was eagerly looking forward to her new job as an analyst with a firm of stockbrokers. She had studied hard to gain her qualifications and had packed a lot of relevant experience into her working life to date. She knew she could do a good job for her new employers and help them to trade more profitably.

When she arrived at their head office all the senior staff were on leave, and a junior showed her to a poky, windowless office in a remote part of the building which she was to share with three other new analysts until alterations to the main office had been completed.

Although trained in computer operation, she had no terminal and had to travel three floors every time she wanted to access the main computer. Thus all her work had to be hand-written and then typed (with many errors) by a typist, which sharply reduced both the quantity and quality of her output. After three days two of the directors returned and she discovered she would be working for both of them. Since their priorities clashed she worked under increasing pressure to satisfy both but received little recognition from either.

Ten months later she had still not been moved into the main office and felt shut off and unappreciated. She applied for and obtained a post with another firm, this time ensuring that her working conditions and treatment would match the effort she was prepared to put into the job.

Six months later her previous employers were still trying to replace her and the profit she had helped them generate.

It seems that often we do everything possible to discourage discretionary effort. If you want to optimise your organisation's performance you will need to understand the main factors that encourage this effort.

You will need to know what managerial philosophies, systems and behaviours will help to create the type of work environment which will cause your employees to want to do the job really well, rather than to do just enough to get by from one pay day to the next. You will need to develop at least a working knowledge of the 'how' and 'why' of people's behaviour at work, without getting too involved in all the research which led us up to the point we are at today.

And this we will start on in the next chapter.

POINTS TO REMEMBER

1. Whether or not people are your business's most valuable asset, they certainly hold the key to your profitability.
2. A key factor in the success or failure of any enterprise is the *motivation* of its people.
3. Motivation can be defined as 'the drive or desire to exert effort'.
4. The effort required to meet a minimum standard of performance is known as *maintenance effort*.
5. The effort required to do a job really well and exceed minimum standards is known as *discretionary effort*.
6. Providing a work environment that encourages effort at the discretionary level is the secret of dynamic people management.

2

Motivation made easy

So far we have agreed that motivation may be defined as *the drive or desire to exert effort*. The amount of effort so generated can be measured on a scale running from the maintenance level, at its lowest ebb, through levels of discretionary effort up to a theoretical maximum level of effort.

We say 'theoretical maximum' deliberately because, in practice, there seems to be almost no limit to what human beings can achieve when highly motivated.

> When Roger Bannister first ran a mile in under four minutes it was considered a tremendous feat. Now it is regarded almost as a necessary qualification for serious 'milers' before competing in national events.

> When Hillary and Tenzing conquered Everest it was a 'nine-day wonder'. Although their names remain in the *Guinness Book of Records* it would be hard to remember all the other, sometimes unlikely, combinations of climbers who have since succeeded.

We can describe anything which contributes to an increase in the drive or desire to exert effort as a *motivator*. Conversely, anything which tends to reduce this drive can be described as a *demotivator*.

If we could define clearly and simply what constitutes motivators and demotivators for all employees we would have solved the problem of motivation for you and everyone else searching for dedicated staff. Unfortunately, however, there is one inescapable fact that has to be faced:

PEOPLE ARE DIFFERENT

No two people have exactly the same genetic make-up (even twins) and no two people respond identically to attempts to encourage them to greater effort. Because of this a vast amount of research has gone into the field of work motivation, and a summary of even the major theories would take up at least the rest of this book.

Certainly no one theory of motivation is adequate to explain all its complexities, nor why an approach which motivates one individual or group of individuals may not work with another. So before we can identify some practical motivators and demotivators, let's look briefly at some of the more popular theories and see if we can draw any practical conclusions from them.

For many years up to about the middle of this century almost all managers believed that people were basically lazy but could be motivated by material rewards. Accordingly, early attempts to improve the productivity or output of people at work were mostly focused on giving people set tasks or quotas and paying them for meeting these. Even fifty years ago 'piece-work' or payment for work completed was a common basis for pay.

Later research, however, began to reveal that people are a great deal more complex and that they are in fact motivated by a variety of interrelated factors. Moreover, different people have different goals and are therefore motivated in different ways. Researchers also began to focus their attention more closely on the work itself, and to realise that to make work meaningful and interesting could increase motivation levels. In other words, all people are not inherently lazy nor do they work purely for money and other material benefits.

Many of the most valuable research findings have been discovered almost by accident, as for example Newton's apple and Fleming's penicillin. Motivation research has benefited similarly.

In the early 1930s a pioneer researcher into motivation was conducting studies into the effect of working conditions on two groups of workers at a large plant in America. One group acted as a control and their conditions remained unchanged except that their output was visibly recorded. The other group was subjected to changes in basic conditions such as lighting, heating, etc.

With each change the output of the second group improved even though in some cases conditions were deteriorating, not improving. To the surprise of the researcher output also improved in the control group although their conditions didn't change at all.

In the end it appeared that both groups were simply responding to the increased interest being shown in them by management. They had been motivated by *recognition*.

To simplify our brief study of the many theories involved we can divide them into three types:

- *People* theories, which are concerned with the individual.
- *Job* theories, relating mainly to the way the job is structured and performed.
- *Organisational* theories, relating to the way the organisation is arranged and managed.

A fourth category may be necessary to cover those theories which relate to more than one of the three types.

People
One of the most popular theories in management circles even today is Maslow's *needs hierarchy*, which has its origins as far back as the 1940s. Maslow proposed that there are basic needs common to all people and that these can be considered as a hierarchy (or series of steps). Once the individual's lower-level needs have been satisfied he then attempts to satisfy the next need in the hierarchy, and so on.

First, man must satisfy his physiological needs, such as food, water and air. For example, a starving man will focus all his efforts on satisfying his need for food and is unlikely to pay much attention to anything else until he has done so. A drowning man strives for air, a thirsty man for water.

Next come the security or safety needs, where again the same principle applies. Even when the person is in no immediate physical danger, these needs can be seen to be active in the form of de-

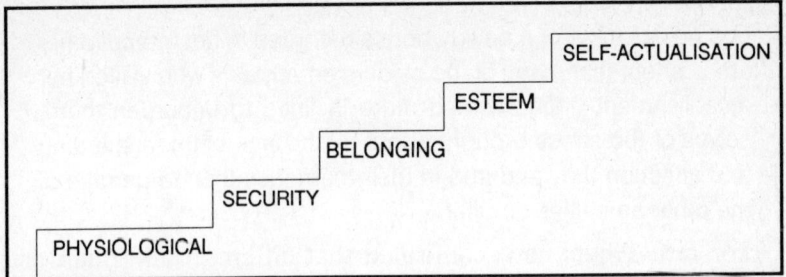

mands for such safeguards as insurance policies, pensions and se-
cure jobs.

Third in the hierarchy comes the need for affection and a sense
of belonging. Wanting to be seen as belonging to a work team is an
example of this in practice.

Then comes the esteem need—the need for both self-esteem and
the esteem of others in the form of recognition and attention.
These lead to a feeling of self-confidence and self-worth. In the
work situation visible status symbols may also help to meet this
need—for example, having a prestige company car or an impressive
job title.

At the highest level in the hierarchy comes the need for self-ac-
tualisation or self-fulfilment. This need can be expressed in the
work situation in a variety of ways, such as being able to make decisions and set one's own objectives.

Although all of us are subject to these basic needs and driven to
fulfil them, their relative importance will vary between people and
also within an individual at any given time. In a confirmed 'loner'
the need for belonging may be relatively weak but his need for esteem may be strong. An individual will try to satisfy that need which
is uppermost at any one time.

Although the need for sexual gratification is considered to be one
of the most basic and powerful drives affecting all animal life including man, even it may take a back seat on occasions.

The proprietress of a bawdy house recorded in her memoirs her amazement that many of the balding enthusiasts who visited her establishment often seemed more inclined to unburden themselves of the stress brought about by the lack of understanding and affection they endured in their marriages than to partake of the other amenities on offer.

Other researchers have confirmed that different individuals are motivated by very different things, depending on their own particular needs. However, whilst Maslow argued for a universal hierarchy of needs, another researcher, McClelland, suggests that people can also be classified into one of three very different categories according to their need for

```
ACHIEVEMENT
POWER
AFFILIATION
```

People with a high need for achievement show a preference for situations in which they are personally responsible for solving problems. They also set challenging yet realistic goals for themselves and are prepared to take risks to achieve them. Because the business environment is ideally suited to meeting these needs, many people with a high need for achievement seek satisfaction in business as entrepreneurs.

People with a high need for power like to influence others and to gain positions of leadership—for example, in the field of politics, or as managers in large organisations.

On the other hand, people with a high need for affiliation are more concerned about relationships with, and the feelings of, other people. They therefore seek jobs where they can interact with others in a friendly way.

These findings suggest that different people are likely to excel or do badly in different jobs. For example, the person with a high need for achievement is likely to be a good entrepreneur but a poor manager because of his preference for taking personal responsibility in solving problems rather than delegating this responsibility to others. Similarly, someone with a high need for power may make a good politician but a poor team member because of his need to dominate others.

If you want to find out which category you belong to there are several well-tried tests you can complete, but these are beyond the scope of this book.

So far we have concentrated on people's needs which they are driven to fulfil in various ways—the drive to fulfil their needs motivating them to expend the effort required to obtain satisfaction. But how do we fulfil these needs in an everyday job of work?

The job

Frederick Hertzberg was probably the researcher who delivered the final blow to the earlier notion that people worked solely for money. Although money still rated highly as a means of fulfilling many basic needs, he found that a satisfying job could meet many of the other needs and thus provide a strong stimulus for expending discretionary effort.

In a series of wide-ranging studies carried on in many parts of the world (including South Africa) he consistently showed that, where a job provided an opportunity to achieve and advance, as well as recognition for the effort expended, motivation increased. Such factors he termed *motivators*.

He also found that job satisfaction and job dissatisfaction are not opposites, and the job characteristics which lead to satisfaction (and work motivation) are quite distinct from those which lead to dissatisfaction. Job dissatisfaction is caused by factors which are separate from the job itself but which exist in the working environment—such as salary, working conditions, and status. Hertzberg refers to these as *hygiene factors*, using the analogy of a hospital which has to maintain a basic level of hygiene if its patients are not to die before being treated.

When these hygiene factors are adequate the individual is not necessarily satisfied (or motivated); it merely means that he is *not dissatisfied* (or demotivated) by them. In other words, their presence at an acceptable level is necessary to ensure that efforts to increase job satisfaction are not undermined.

Job satisfaction, on the other hand, is the result of factors which relate directly to the job itself—the motivators—and by building more of these motivators into any job (even menial tasks) the motivation of the people concerned can be increased. This process Hertzberg referred to as *job enrichment*.

A simple example of job enrichment quoted by Hertzberg describes giving a group of office cleaners the responsibility for drawing up their own budget for cleaning materials and monitoring their expenditure on these items on an ongoing basis. Earlier writers on work motivation would probably have rated this experiment as having little chance of success since it merely increased responsibility without any increase in rewards. However, Hertzberg found in many such experiments that levels of motivation and productivity actually increased significantly under such conditions.

Much work along similar lines has been done in the automobile industry in Sweden, Japan and, more recently, in the USA where small autonomous workgroups are made responsible for all aspects of producing finished assemblies. The basic principle of removing demotivating working conditions and increasing job satisfaction forms a basis for many other studies on the subject.

The organisation

A great deal of work has been done in the area of identifying which management or supervisory style contributes best to a motivated workforce; perhaps the best-known writer in this field is Likert, who identifies four different systems or styles of management:

> EXPLOITATIVE AUTHORITATIVE
> BENEVOLENT AUTHORITATIVE
> CONSULTATIVE
> PARTICIPATIVE

Exploitative authoritative managers treat all employees as hired hands without human rights or needs. The best (or worst) examples include 19th-century mill owners, colliery owners and ships' masters. Unfortunately the type is not confined to history, and there are still many managers who would like to model their businesses on the good ship *Bounty*, forgetting that its seemingly unassailable master, Captain Bligh, eventually found himself cast adrift in a lifeboat!

Benevolent authoritative managers abound, particularly in this country, where the need to support a large and often poorly educated workforce creates a strong tendency to paternalism. Very often well-meaning attempts to educate managers in human relations result in an intensification of this tendency to *do unto others as you would be done by* rather than as *they* would prefer to be treated.

Likert suggests that the more effective approach lies in the remaining two styles.

Consultative management means simply that employees are consulted wherever possible in matters that affect them so that management will at least know their probable reaction to proposed

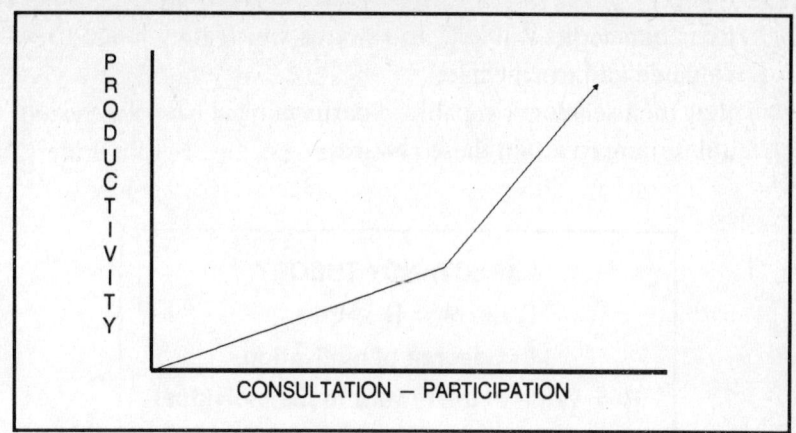

developments. The rapid strengthening of the power of the trade unions is forcing greater recourse to this method whether we like it or not.

Finally, *participative* managers follow two basic principles:

1. They encourage supportive relationships—ie those which build a sense of personal worth and importance.
2. They develop group decision-making and supervision—as opposed to the traditional approach where managers deal with these matters on the basis of each subordinate separately.

Extensive research using this model has shown that high-producing departments or organisations almost invariably make use of the latter two systems, whereas low-producing units use the first two. Furthermore, organisations which have moved towards participative management have effected considerable increases in productivity as well as better labour relations. Reverting to the first system invariably has the reverse effect.

Other related theories

A number of writers have contributed to what is known as *expectancy theory*. Simply stated, this says that people will be highly motivated when they believe that:

- their behaviour will lead to rewards which they judge to be valuable and worthwhile;
- they themselves are capable of performing at a level which enables them to attain these rewards.

EXPECTANCY THEORY

$$M = R \times P$$

M = degree of motivation

R = value of the reward to the individual

P = perceived probability of attainment

Highly motivated people believe that they will achieve their desired rewards through their efforts. In practical terms, this implies that desirable behaviour will occur only when it is rewarded relative to undesirable behaviour. Whilst this seems to be a matter of basic common sense, it is surprising how often it is not applied in organisations.

Mary worked hard at secretarial school and it was no surprise that she passed top of her class. She had no difficulty in getting a job in the typing pool of a large multinational company.

When she joined, the assistant personnel manager told her that the level of her starting salary took into account the strong recommendation that accompanied her from her school. She also assured Mary that future increases would be linked to her level of productivity.

Mary settled in well and soon got accustomed to their way of working. Later she took a word processing course at her local technical college in her spare time, and began to tackle some of the more difficult jobs for the advertising department. Pretty soon she was getting all the tricky jobs and often had to stay late to get them done while the other typists went off at the usual time. She didn't mind because she enjoyed the work and remembered what the manager had said about productivity-related pay.

Talking to one of the other typists one day in the washroom she discovered that her pay was the same as that which the other typists were getting, and that everyone started at the same level. Although surprised, she wasn't upset because she was sure that she would get a good increase at the year end.

Came the day when her pay cheque was accompanied by a letter thanking her for her excellent work and advising that her salary had been raised by 10 %. She was delighted and felt that the extra effort had been worthwhile.

Later she learned through the washroom telegraph that all the typists had been given the same increase.

After the shock wore off she decided that she would not take more than her fair share of work and would definitely not work late anymore. After a while she became so bored with her job that she left and secured a more satisfying job as a private secretary.

Simply rewarding good work with more work is an example of what another researcher, Skinner, calls *negative reinforcement*. One of the most controversial of all the early behavioural scientists, he conducted experiments with a variety of animals (including his own one-year-old son) to prove his theory that desirable behaviour could be encouraged by rewards (or positive reinforcement) but was discouraged when its performance elicited unpleasant results (negative reinforcement).

Taking his experiments further he demonstrated that rewarding every performance rapidly led to its becoming expected so that eventually no work was done unless rewarded. However, when rewards were given only occasionally (intermittent reinforcement) the prospect of being rewarded sooner or later spurred the subject to even greater effort, like people constantly pressing a lift button when the lift is slow in coming. Similarly, the possibility of an unpleasant result at some unexpected time would be sufficient to deter performance, like the *don't drink and drive* campaign.

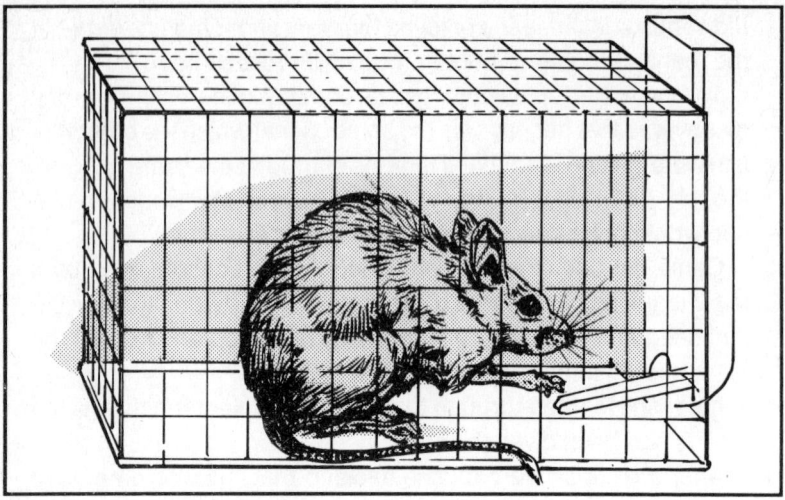

As the story of Mary showed, many businesses are unaware of the need to provide positive reinforcement and to avoid negative reinforcement if productivity is to be kept at a high level. Many are also, perhaps understandably, unaware of the many other complex theories on the factors which affect work performance. However, there are some simple rules which will help all managers to improve the motivation of their employees.

POINTS TO REMEMBER

DO

- recognise that people are different
- try to understand their individual needs
- develop satisfying jobs—interesting and challenging
- let employees participate in setting performance standards
- ensure prompt feedback of results
- provide positive reinforcement when standards are met

DON'T

- neglect the hygiene factors
- give only negative reinforcement

3

Whose job is it?

The quick and easy answer to that question is that motivation is a part of every manager's job.

However, having read this far you are probably already beginning to feel a bit daunted by the wide range of tasks which seem to face managers in developing and maintaining a high level of motivation amongst their employees. After all, managers are busy people with direct and pressing responsibilities for bottom-line results. Where do you find the time to worry about these seemingly less urgent and less critical problems?

You will often hear it said by managers that all this motivation stuff is fine in large companies which can afford to employ personnel specialists to take care of it, leaving operating managers to get on with their primary job of making profits. But, they will add, in most companies (including their own) most managers simply have too many other important things to worry about. It may be all very well in theory but time just isn't available in practice to implement these fancy ideas.

Finding time for people management

There is, unfortunately, no simple answer to the problem of finding or making enough time but it will help if we begin by recognising some important principles:

1. A well-known definition of management is that it is 'the work
    of deciding objectives and then ensuring they are achieved
    through the efforts of others'. The words in italics are the key to
    management. If the objectives are achieved without the involve-
    ment of others then the work is that of an operator, not a
    manager.

    It follows that the job of directing, controlling and motivating
    the efforts of others is inescapably a major responsibility of
    anyone who aspires to the status of manager.

2. Earlier we spoke of the *people* resource. A manager has many
    resources allocated to him to help him achieve his objectives—
    money, materials, machinery, facilities and people. It is his re-
    sponsibility to ensure they are all used in the most productive
    manner possible. A machine without sufficient power and lu-
    brication will produce no more than a person without motiva-
    tion—both resources need to be managed effectively.

3. No manager can abdicate responsibility for *people management*
    to personnel officers, human resource managers or anyone
    else. Such specialists, if they exist in his organisation, can, how-

ever, most certainly help him by developing sound hygiene in such areas as job specifications, selection, training, remuneration and administration.

But the ultimate responsibility of effectively managing his people resource remains that of the operating manager.

So there is no escaping the fundamental fact that any manager who wants, or needs to increase the productivity of his people through better motivation has no alternative but to find or make available time to do so.

Many surveys, conducted all over the world, of how managers spend their time show that middle managers generally spend more time on operating tasks than on management tasks.

All managers have some operating tasks to perform and the load will vary with their position in the organisation, but all must somehow set aside sufficient time to do the essential management tasks inherent in any management job.

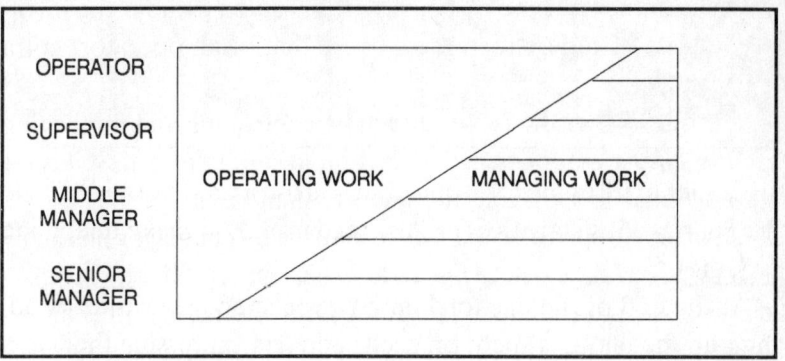

Let's get MAD

The simplest way to make time available for managing your people is to start a MAD programme. It's not quite as loony as it sounds because MAD stands for

```
MEASURE
ANALYSE
DELEGATE
```

which are the three steps of the programme.

The first step is to *measure* how you actually spend your time now, by recording what you do every five minutes throughout the day. Use some pre-prepared sheets like this:

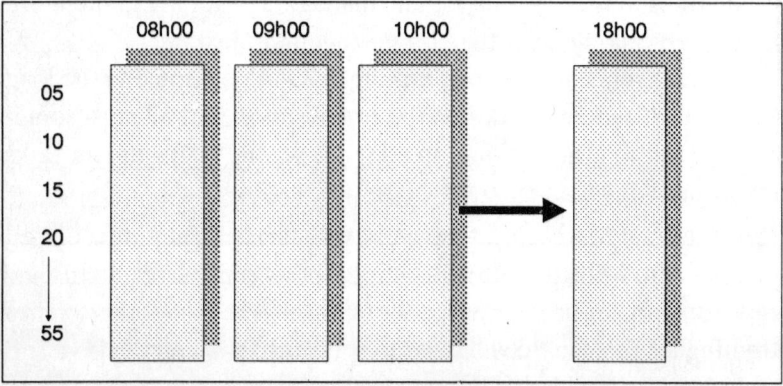

It's easier to fill in the form quickly if you use a predetermined code for your various activities (eg A = read mail, B = make telephone call, etc).

At the end of the day total up how you spend your time by adding up the minutes spent on each code and expressing them as a percentage of your working day. If you worked an eight-hour day your record would start off looking something like this:

A = 15 min
$\therefore 15/480 \times 100 = 3\%$

B = 45 min
$\therefore 45/480 \times 100 = 9\%$

Keeping this record for several days over a representative period gives you a clear picture of how you spend your days.

When you have recovered from the shock and stopped making excuses to yourself for the picture revealed ('it was just a bad week') you can move on to the next step. This is to analyse the work into (*a*) tasks that only you can do and *(b)* tasks that you can delegate to someone else.

TASKS I DO	CAN BE DONE BY ME ONLY	CAN BE DONE BY (NAME)	IMMEDIATELY	AFTER TRAINING

Once you have answered the questions honestly you are ready to take the final MAD step. The work you can delegate immediately you pass on, with suitable instructions, performance standards and reporting procedures, to your subordinates. The work that requires training a subordinate will have to wait until you can devise a formal plan to train him or her and get co-operation and agreement. We'll go into more detail as to how this can be done in a later chapter.

A survey of ninety managers in three companies revealed a surprising number who had more potential than the job required.

- Company A 43 %
- Company B 34 %
- Company C 50 %

A properly conducted MAD programme could have tapped this hidden resource.

There are a couple of things you should bear in mind before you get MAD:

1. The subordinate(s) concerned may need to follow a similar process to enable them to find the time to handle the additional work. Remember the story of the managing director who told the consultant that he knew the MAD programme was working because the tea lady had just had a nervous breakdown!

2. The process can be highly motivating to your subordinates if you choose the tasks to be delegated wisely, ensure that they are properly equipped to handle each task and, if appropriate, are also rewarded for undertaking additional responsibilities.

And once the programme is running do not forget your original objective—which was to make time to manage your people more effectively. Unless your are very firm this additional time you have won for yourself through a considerable amount of effort will be whittled away by other, non-people-related matters.

The MD was very worried about the Small Machine Shop.

Although titled 'Small' it was by no means small in importance, forming a vital link in the production chain. Its manager Pat Hines had been with the company for many years and had virtually grown up in the SM shop, starting as a lathe operator and working his way up to foreman, until a year ago when he was promoted to the position of manager.

Personnel had been trying to get him to attend the management development course which was offered to all newly appointed managers, but so far without success. He always said he was too busy to go back to school and, in any case, what could some university drop-out (a libellous reference to the company training officer) teach him about running the shop he'd spent most of his working life getting to know?

Busy he certainly was. Always there first in the morning, out in the machine room checking on the foremen and making sure the rush jobs got out, he wasn't above taking off his jacket and tackling a difficult piece of machine setting himself. His office light burned far into the night as he struggled to catch up on all the paper work that piled up during the day. But in spite of his heroic efforts there were frequent crises and production delays.

In due course the years of endless pressure, snatched meals and chain-smoking took their inevitable toll, and he was rushed into hospital after suffering a severe heart attack. He survived, but his doctor insisted he take three months off work to recover fully.

Not without some misgivings the MD decided to put a management trainee, Pete Marais, in to hold the fort until Pat Hines was able to return to work. Although he lacked practical experience, Pete had done well in business studies at university and was showing ability to get on well with people in difficult situations. He'd certainly need that to get on with the old hands in the SM shop.

During his first week Pete took a passive role, allowing the seemingly unending tide of detail to flow over him. His production clerk expected him to check every work order that came in and personally to schedule the work. His storeman wanted him to OK every requisition before he would issue the material required by the foremen and to check every receipt. His secretary dropped the mail on his desk as it arrived and waited for him to dictate replies to every memo personally. The foremen were even more demanding, wanting his approval for everything they did, from setting up a machine to giving a late-comer a verbal warning. Whenever he asked why they came to him he got the same reply: 'Pat liked to keep his finger on things.'

At the end of the second week Pete felt he was ready to start making some small changes in the role he was expected to play. He called his staff together on Friday afternoon – they warned him all work would stop in their absence – and spent half an hour explaining that management wasn't a one-man show, but that they all had a part to play if the job was to run smoothly.

Then he outlined to them the decisions he thought they could take without reference to him, those where they should tell him what they had done, and those few where they should get his prior approval. After some discussion he got them to accept responsibility for the bulk of their daily jobs, reserving to himself only the critical decisions affecting changes to the schedule and disciplining and employing staff.

At first they weren't too happy to take decisions, and continued to cover themselves by telling him what they were doing. But little by little they gained confidence and, except for a few near disasters, started to manage their own jobs properly.

Rid of the burden of detail, Pete was able to spend time overhauling the work planning procedures, which he had identified as the cause of previous problems in the shop. By doing so he was able to eliminate most of the delays which had formerly plagued production.

He also spent some time wondering what Pat Hines would do when he returned to work and hoped that the shock of the new management techniques he had introduced wouldn't precipitate another heart attack.

Where do you start?

You've undoubtedly heard the catch-phrase *'managing by walking around'* (MBWA), first publicised by Peters and Waterman in their best seller *In Search of Excellence*. Many of the organisations they researched in their landmark study considered that MBWA contributed significantly to their success.

So perhaps a very good place to begin is simply to spend a bit more time with your people—unless you are one of those rare managers who already knows his staff well.

We do not suggest that you waste your time and theirs in idle chatter about last Saturday's rugby or football game or the latest soapie on TV. Nor do we suggest that, like Pat Hines, you spend the time doing the job for them.

What we do suggest is that you can use some of this time very productively by simply talking informally about the job and the person doing it.

- Ask how he feels about the job and whether he is experiencing any particular difficulties.
- Find out if he has any ideas for improving productivity or making the job easier.
- Try to find out what makes him 'tick'—what aspects of the job he likes and which he doesn't.

Remember that two of the cardinal lessons we learned in Chapter 2 were that people are different, and that they respond positively or negatively to different things. So while you're talking to them ask yourself: 'What can I do to encourage *this* person to put in that discretionary effort which will help him progress from only adequate to excellent performance (or help him maintain his present level if he is already an outstanding performer)?'

For example—how does he like to be supervised? Does he require constant guidance (common to a newly appointed employee), or does he prefer to be left to get on with the job once he understands what is required of him?

Later in this book we shall be dealing with a number of formal techniques for establishing these, such as appraisal interviews, training needs analyses, and so on. But these will only be really effective if they are based on a sound knowledge of and relationship with the person concerned, which has been built up through a series of less formal discussions and meetings such as we are suggesting here. Where the person concerned happens to be of another race or colour you will probably have to put extra effort into breaking down barriers of language and culture.

At the lower levels of the organisation relatively wide spans of control make for large workgroups and this may make it difficult to get to know every worker well. Here too the barriers of language and culture are likely to create problems in most South African organisations. But there can be no other area in the organisation where good communication is
(*a*) more important, and
(*b*) more sadly neglected
and where its absence costs so much in real terms.

Communication between management and worker at this level has been very aptly described as *a struggle for the hearts and minds of the workforce*. Certainly it is a struggle we are in real danger of losing unless we take some positive action to breach some of the barriers to communication.

Consider for a moment the working life of the average black worker:

- His normal day begins well before daybreak and ends long after dark.
- He can spend anything up to four or five hours travelling to and from work.
- He is often poorly paid with few fringe benefits.
- He has little or no idea of how the business operates—where funds come from, how money is spent, how profits are used.
- His level of education probably means he has few if any prospects of advancement.
- His supervisor is probably white and in all likelihood does not speak his language.
- He is never told anything about the company or how it is doing by anyone in authority—he relies on the 'grapevine' to keep himself informed.
- He receives little or no feedback on his own performance except for reprimands when he does something wrong.

Under such conditions is it truly surprising to find that the workforce at this level is unmotivated and uninterested, doing just enough work to keep out of trouble and displaying little, if any, discretionary effort? The real surprise would be to find anything different!

The ability radically to change many of the factors—sociopolitical, economic, etc—giving rise to the type of scenario described above lies beyond the average manager, so discussion thereof is beyond the scope of this book. But think for a moment what a difference it could make to communication and morale in your organisation alone if someone in authority just took the trouble to talk to that worker on a regular basis, using some simple textbook guidelines:

- giving him some encouragement and praise for work well done

- telling him how he's doing and how the company (or his department) is doing
- finding out what he likes and dislikes about his job
- seeing whether it is possible to make his work more interesting for him.

Unrealistic? Not at all. A number of organisations have managed to achieve all these things with remarkable gains in productivity as a result—higher output of work, less absenteeism, fewer cases of employees coming late to work.

Why not try it, even in a small section of your operation? It will cost you nothing and you will almost certainly be pleasantly surprised at the results.

Some popular misconceptions expressed by members of the workforce:

1. The business pays money to the Government (taxes); therefore it is part of the Government.
2. The Government tells the company how much to pay us.
3. The managing director and his other managers take the money (profits) home in their cases (briefcases) every night.
4. The money for wages comes from the bank. If they wanted to pay us more they could get more from the bank.
5. The company can afford to pay us more because it has just bought a new Mercedes-Benz for the manager.
6. If we work harder the company will make more money and will buy more cars for the managers.

The role of the personnel department

In a small company the managers have to share all the 'people work' between them because there is no one else, except perhaps a secretary or time-clerk, to help them. However, as companies grow, and particularly as they begin to recognise how much depends on the people resource, they employ specialist managers to help them look after it. How can they do this without infringing on the essential close relationships we have been talking about?

In Chapter 1 we showed diagrammatically how the responsibilities are shared between the operating managers and the supporting personnel function. Here is another view of the same diagram.

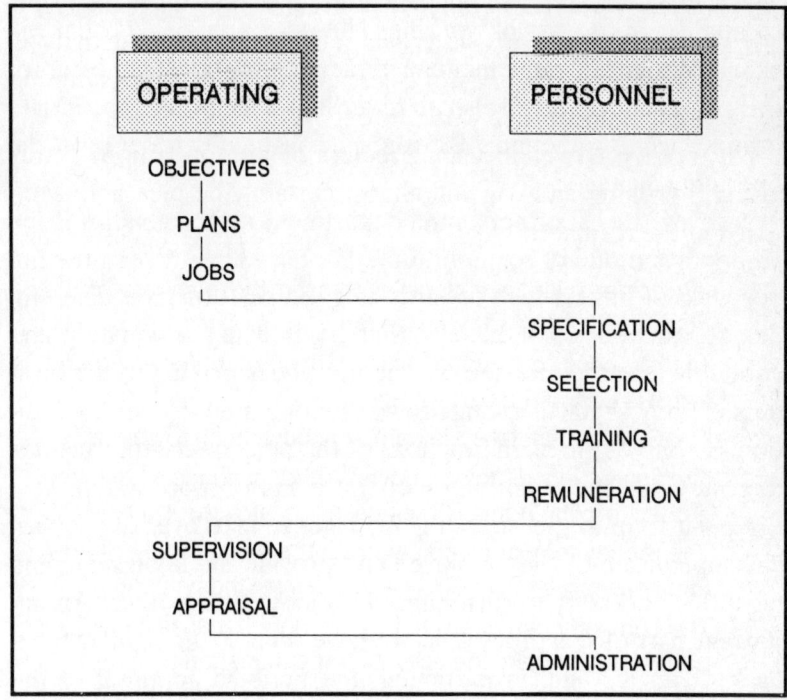

This shows that each has a distinct role in the creation and maintenance of well-motivated employees, although these roles are closely interwoven.

The operating manager's prime responsibility is to set clear objectives based on the organisation's mission, and then to formulate plans for their achievement. These plans will determine the size, shape and number of jobs involved in reaching the objectives, and consequently realising the mission.

At this stage the personnel department will help to draw up specifications for the people needed and will start the process of recruiting and selecting suitable people. The final choice is made by the operating manager who is going to be responsible for managing them.

The chosen recruits will need some sort of introduction to the company and its ways of working. The personnel department will usually design and implement an induction programme to cater for this general need. It will also on request provide other appropriate training while sometimes leaving specialist skills training to the operating manager.

Next on the list of personnel department responsibilities is the all-important one of remuneration. We have already seen the importance of linking high rewards to good performance. The employee who does not believe that he is being adequately and equitably rewarded for the contribution he is making to the business is likely to start looking elsewhere for a more rewarding position. So one of the main functions of the personnel department is to ensure that the organisation operates a fair reward system.

Now it is up to the operating manager to take over the day-to-day supervision of the employee and provide the knowledge and incentive necessary to turn him into a motivated worker. An important part of this process, as we have seen, is the regular feedback of results and, in particular, the periodic appraisal of the employee as an individual. Although the operating manager will carry out this appraisal, the personnel department will often provide the framework for the appraisal interview and train the manager in the necessary techniques.

Finally, to prevent the motivated employee from becoming demotivated by any absence of the necessary hygiene factors, the personnel department will develop and operate the systems and tools which the organisation needs to develop and maintain a motivated workforce. These may include equitable people policies and procedures, conditions of service, employee benefit programmes and industrial relations systems.

In addition an effectively managed organisation will ensure that there are development programmes available which help employees to reach their full potential in the organisation rather than be forced to look elsewhere to achieve this. This means proper promotion and career planning systems as well as training and development programmes to prepare the employee to meet the requirements of the new position.

Personnel department – friend or foe?
By now it should be clear that the personnel function should not be regarded as an expensive luxury but rather as an integral part of the company's efforts to enhance its profitability through the effective use of its people resource. In order to fill this role it needs to operate in close liaison and co-operation with the operating management, and to provide the systems and skills which will enable the development and maintenance of high levels of employee motivation.

For their part, operating managers should make the fullest possible use of the expertise available to them and play their part in the development of new and meaningful procedures and policies.

In the absence of a personnel specialist the operating manager has little option but to carry out the functions himself. He will find the work rewarding but time-consuming, and will need to develop delegation skills into a fine art if he is to be able to provide the ideal support for his workforce.

Should you decide to go it alone at least this little book will enable you to avoid the deepest pitfalls.

POINTS TO REMEMBER
1. Management is the work of establishing objectives and then ensuring they are achieved through the efforts of others.
2. All operating managers are ultimately responsible for the people resources allocated to them.
3. Motivating people requires time and effort.
4. Measuring, analysing and delegating work (MAD) will provide the time necessary to motivate your people.
5. Time spent in building sound employee relationships will pay off a hundredfold.

4

Hire and higher performance

Have you ever stopped to think how much it costs an organisation to replace someone who cannot adequately perform the work for which he was originally hired?

First there is the cost of lost performance. For a rank-and-file employee it is fairly easy to add up the cost of all the substandard work he has done which led up to the decision to get rid of him. For a manager or supervisor, or someone who influenced the business in other ways, the cost of substandard performance is infinitely greater, harder to assess, and includes the cost of his manager's time spent correcting the foul-ups.

To this must be added the cost of separating the departing employee—whatever is paid in lieu of notice or to hasten the departure. Nowadays dismissing an unsatisfactory employee is no longer as straightforward as it used to be, and many an employer has found himself defending his actions in the Industrial Court with all the legal and other costs that this can entail—even sometimes adverse publicity for the organisation.

In addition we must take into account the costs of finding a replacement. Apart from the direct costs involved in advertising the position or paying consultants' fees, there is also the time of the people concerned in arranging and conducting the interviews, and possibly the travelling costs of at least some of the candidates. Once the selection has been made there may be relocation expenses, the cost of inducting the new employee into the company, as well as the cost of his salary for the weeks—or months—it may take him to become a fully productive member of staff.

Because many of these are hidden costs they are often over-looked, but they can amount to several weeks' wages in the case of lower-level employees, or the equivalent of six months' salary or more for a senior executive.

SEPARATION LOSSES	
Performance lost	R . . .
Separation payout	R . . .
Legal costs	R . . .
Advertising	R . . .
Interview costs	R . . .
Relocation costs	R . . .
Induction costs	R . . .
Unproductive time	R . . .
TOTAL LOSS	R . . .

Next time you have the unpleasant task of terminating someone's employment use this list to record the losses incurred and then think how they are going to be made up or, better still, how to avoid them in the future.

Harry Woods wasn't looking forward to interviewing Peter Harmon later today. He didn't like having to sack anyone but Peter had really been living on borrowed time for many months now.

It wasn't that he deliberately sabotaged the regional office where he was in charge—it was just that he didn't seem to be able to cope with the load which the new product launch had imposed on everyone. Goodness knows how many customers they had lost during the breakdown of the whole recording system in Peter's region, which he was supposed to supervise.

Harry had spent a lot of time with Peter to help him to settle into the job and, when things started to go wrong, had tried to counsel him on several occasions. Although Peter said he understood the problem and that he would fix it, he never did, and now the MD had told Harry to 'fix it' — permanently.

Harry remembered hiring him two years before. Peter had seemed well enough qualified for the job — he'd been in lots of similar situations before. Perhaps that was the trouble — he'd been in too many situations before. Harry recalled having had some doubts about his record but he'd seemed the best of those who had applied at the time. Perhaps he should have taken a bit more time even though everyone was in such a hurry to get on with the new product. Oh well! better get it over with and start again.

When you consider the potential cost of employing an unsatisfactory worker it is easy to appreciate that staff selection is one of the more important skills in the effective manager's repertoire. Selecting the right people to do the job is absolutely critical to the success of the enterprise and, unless this is done properly, subsequent attempts by management to maximise performance will meet with at best limited success.

Yet despite the very substantial costs incurred through poor selection decisions, many managers still continue to decide on the suitability or otherwise of even senior-level staff on the flimsiest information—often gained during one brief and poorly conducted interview.

Possibly one of the main reasons for this strange behaviour is the widely held fallacy that successful staff selection is some kind of gift or knack, rather than a skill which can be learned. Beware the manager who boasts that he is a 'good judge of character' and that he can sum up anyone in a matter of minutes! The human personality is extremely complex, as any psychologist will tell you, and snap judgements of this nature have little chance of being accurate.

Staff selection, like nearly every other management task, is a skill which can be learned. Here are five simple steps which any manager can follow and which will improve his selection skills immediately.

1. Define the job to be done

Perhaps the most common error in staff selection is to decide what kind of person is required before the job itself has been carefully defined. This almost invariably results in a mismatch between the requirements of the job and the person selected to perform it. In most cases where this approach is used the tendency is to look for someone who is overqualified for the position and thus more costly to hire and more likely *not* to fit the job. So the first step is to draw up a **job description**.

In its most basic form a job description need be no more than a statement of

> **WHAT HAS TO BE ACHIEVED (RESULT)**
> **HOW IT IS ACHIEVED (TASK)**

However basic its form, it is vital that thought is given to expressing these two components as clearly and as definitely as possible, since the job description will be used not only for selection but also, as we shall see later, as the basis for other managerial activities, such as review, appraisal and remuneration.

The first step is to decide the **purpose** of the position—why it was created, what it was created to achieve. This will help us to think of it as *achieving* rather than *doing*. Unless we state clearly what we want the position to achieve, the holder can beaver away all day and yet make no positive contribution to the organisation's objectives. A typical statement of **purpose** for a clerical position may be:

'To ensure that all transactions are correctly invoiced.'

This is why the position was created and exists and, presumably, contributes to achieving the organisation's objectives.

Once the purpose has been defined we can start to list the **results** we want from it. Here we must try to list results rather than the activities that lead up to them.

For example:
'1. All movements out of the store are correctly invoiced (result).'
Rather than:
'1. Invoice all materials issued (activity).'

Having defined all the important issues or *key* results we expect the position to achieve, we can list under each one the **tasks** (activities) necessary to achieve it.

JOB DESCRIPTION

TITLE: Invoice clerk

PURPOSE: To ensure all transactions are correctly invoiced

KEY RESULTS AND TASKS:
1. All movements out of the store are correctly invoiced.

1.1   Check part no and description of each item.

1.2   Enter quantity, part no and description on invoice.

1.3   Enter unit price from price list and extend. . . . etc

Note that each task description starts with an active verb, eg 'check', 'enter', and should describe clearly what has to be done to achieve the required result. Although this logical approach to writing a job description may take a little longer than a rough list of duties, it will save time and effort later in the process.

2. Develop a person specification

The job description forms the basis of the next step in the process, which is to develop a **person specification**. Like job descriptions these can be very sophisticated and complex documents, but a simple and practical format could look like this:

PERSON SPECIFICATION

JOB TITLE

AGE RANGE

MINIMUM EDUCATIONAL QUALIFICATION

OTHER FORMAL TRAINING REQUIRED

PREVIOUS WORK EXPERIENCE

– ESSENTIAL

– PREFERABLE ADDITIONAL

PERSONAL ATTRIBUTES (eg initiative, ability
to influence others, good communications skills)

The list of personal attributes should be kept to a minimum—certainly no more than four or five—and should be capable of verification. It is also important to ensure that whoever is responsible for the selection decision is clear as to the precise meaning of these. For example, does 'good communicator' refer to verbal or written communications, or both? In which language(s) will he need to communicate?

The person specification is drawn up from the job description and is used as a guide for the person(s) involved in the recruiting and selection process. Some common errors to avoid in drawing up a person specification are:

1. Don't overstate the requirements for the position. It is import-ant to take a realistic view of these, bearing in mind the point raised in Chapter 2 that most people perform best when given a job which stretches them a little and presents them with a re-alistic challenge. A person who is overqualified for the position in terms of formal education, training or previous experience will in all likelihood become bored with the work after a very short time.

2. Don't assume that the present or previous holder of the job necessarily had the ideal background for the position—espe-cially if he is or was a good performer in it. In such cases it is important to consider which particular attributes were the rea-son for his success rather than simply assuming that what is re-quired is a carbon copy.

3. Don't neglect to prepare a specification for routine or unskilled jobs. Even though it may be a very elementary job, selecting against a list of basic requirements—physical as well as men-tal—will help to maintain or improve the quality of the work-force. It is unwise to leave the quality of this basic resource input to the personal prejudices of an unskilled assessor.

3. Eliminate non-starters

Once the vacancy has been advertised in some way and applications have been received, some sort of screening procedure is necessary to produce a **short list** of candidates worth the time and effort re-quired to assess their suitability.

This is normally done by having them complete some form of ap-plication which calls for key information in the areas listed in the specification. Choice of those candidates warranting further inves-tigation can usually be made on the basis of possession of the attributes listed in the specification—those possessing them qualifying for more detailed consideration and those lacking any of them being rejected. A more sophisticated approach could entail rating each attribute as essential or desirable, and rejecting only those who do not possess all the essential attributes.

If you are fortunate enough to have a personnel department in your organisation one (or more) of its specialists will usually take responsibility for this screening, and will often carry out preliminary interviews as well, to produce a short list. However, the final choice will be yours and this means that the next step is to—

4. Conduct planned interviews

This is undoubtedly the most difficult phase of the selection process, even assuming that steps 1, 2 and 3 above have been properly completed. (If they have not it is simpler and probably just as effective to toss a coin or draw straws to decide which is the best candidate!) However, like all management work it becomes easier if you follow a logical method. Here is a practicable one: Get ready ... Steady ... Go!

Get ready ...
Always prepare thoroughly before meeting the candidate—it's just as important that he forms a good impression of you as you should of him, particularly in these days when vital skills are getting scarce. So your interview should give the impression of caring efficiency.

Examine his CV or application form thoroughly, deciding in which particular areas he appears to meet, exceeds or fails to meet the minimum requirements of the person specification. Concentrate on possible areas of weakness, and draft questions you will need to ask to obtain more information.

Develop an interview plan but make it flexible so as to allow you to explore other areas which may arise during the course of the interview. Don't be afraid to refer to your plan openly as you go along, and tick off each item as it is covered.

Try to ensure that you are not interrupted during the interview itself even if this means moving to another room or office. Make sure you have enough time to handle the interview properly—remember the possible cost to the organisation if you scrimp it.

Steady . . .
Begin the interview by putting the candidate at ease. Interviews are always stressful events for the person being interviewed, and this stress can be increased by the interviewer who launches straight into the proceedings in a brusque, official manner. Remember that while some stress is inevitable and will often put the candidate on his mettle, too much may well cause him to give a falsely unfavourable picture of himself. It will help if you spend the first few minutes in friendly conversation, trying to find some common ground.

Pay some attention to the seating arrangements. A desk is often perceived as a barrier by the interviewee. Try to avoid this by sitting

on the same side as he if possible or, better still, by sitting at right angles to each other at a coffee table. Show consideration by asking him about any time constraints he may have.

Go!
Move into the interview proper by outlining the course it will follow. For example, tell him that you intend to start by asking some questions about his previous experience and qualifications, and then he'll have a chance to ask questions about the job and the organisation. Indicate whether this is a final interview or merely a preliminary one.

It is important to get the applicant to do most of the talking. Some interviewers, who presumably can't get a word in edgeways at home, often use the interview as a heaven-sent opportunity to unload on their favourite topic to a captive audience! Indeed, some placement consultants actually teach candidates to encourage the interviewer to talk, thereby taking the heat off themselves. Obviously the less a candidate talks, the less you can find out about him, so it is important to let him hold the floor and to encourage him to expand on the bare facts you have in the summary you prepared before the meeting.

One technique used by skilled interviewers with great success is

---

SILENCE

Even the strongest candidate will break down after a few seconds of silence and start to talk, giving the interviewer the opportunity to guide the conversation into areas he wants to explore.

You may have to probe to get him to talk about any weak areas you have noted in his application or that might have come up in the interview. It's particularly important to get him to fill in any periods that are not covered by his list of previous activities—there is usually a reason for not bringing them to your attention, eg long periods of unemployment of frequent breaks in service.

Try to avoid questions which can be answered simply 'yes' or 'no'. Instead, when exploring areas which are hard to define, ask open-ended questions. For example, instead of asking 'Are you decisive?'—to which he is obviously going to answer 'Yes', telling you nothing—it is better to ask something like 'Can you give me an example of a difficult decision you've had to make in your present job and how you dealt with it?' This forces him to be specific and will enable you to judge for yourself whether he is decisive or not.

When you have all the information you want, or as much as you think you are going to get, wind up the interview by thanking him, and telling him what the next stage will be and when he can expect a decision to be made.

Finally, make sure you have recorded all the information you planned to get and sum up your impressions of the candidate in terms of the person specification for the position.

5. Decide

Did we say that interviewing was the most difficult part of selection? We should have qualified this statement because many managers find the most difficult and worrying part to be the final decision on whom to select. Bearing in mind what we have said about the cost of a wrong decision, we can hardly blame them for being somewhat apprehensive. However, if you handle it logically, as you do any other long-term decisions made in the course of your job, you won't have too much trouble.

The first step in any decision-making process is to list those candidates you are considering who have passed the screening process so far. The list should state how each one meets the criteria included in the specification. You may find it helpful to rate each

SELECTION CRITERIA

POSITION: *Asst. Manager*   NAME: *J. Bloggs*

	RATING	SCORE
Age	10	10
Education	20	15
Other Training	20	15
Experience	30	20
Personal Attributes	20	15
TOTAL:	100	75

criterion (for ease of comparison, let the total be 100) and then to score each candidate against the rating, like this:

You may wish to include other criteria—for example, availability, resettlement costs, business contacts, etc. Adjust your ratings accordingly so that they still add up to 100. The choice will now be a matter of finding who has the highest score, but before you finally decide you have to do two more things.

First you need to check up on any **references** he has supplied. It's surprising how many managers overlook this potentially very useful source of supplementary information on candidates. Obviously there are dangers in accepting the opinions of others who may not be able to take an unbiased view of the person concerned, but nevertheless the benefits usually outweigh the dangers, particularly if you happen to know the referee.

Although a candidate will often offer written references, these are usually so non-committal as to have little value and, if highly laudatory, are always a bit suspect. It is far better where possible to speak to the person concerned, either face to face if you can, otherwise by telephone. When talking to a referee remember that people seldom like to run down others, and therefore you'll have to listen carefully not only to *what* is said but also to *how* it is said (ie confidently, enthusiastically, hesitantly or diffidently, where the person is obviously choosing his words with care to avoid committing himself). It is equally as important to note what is *not* said. Generally it is better to try to control the interview by asking a series of specific questions regarding the candidate's performance on the job rather than to encourage the referee to discuss such intangibles as character and personality, which at best are subjective assessments.

Secondly, it is advisable to test your decision by consulting with someone else in the organisation who is likely to have to interact with the successful candidate. You can do this by having your colleague review the application and your notes and assessment or, preferably, by having him sit in on an interview. If you have done your job correctly it is unlikely that your colleague will disagree vigorously with your decision, but should this occur you would be well advised to review the matter.

Now you can finally go ahead and make your decision, confident in the knowledge that you have done everything possible to ensure that the chosen candidate will be able to perform well in the job specified by the job description with which you started the whole process.

Insider out or outsider in?
Sometimes selection of candidates can be complicated by the need to consider existing employees. After all, when we discussed motivation we mentioned rewards for outstanding performance. What greater reward can there be than promotion or, conversely, what greater demotivator can there be than being overlooked?

When Andre first joined Crypto Corporation's northern region as a trainee salesman 16 years ago they gave him the most difficult territory they had. It was spread over a large geographical area which was developing rapidly and called for high mileages and long hours to cover it properly.

In spite of his lack of training he did well and recovered some of the ground lost by the previous salesman, who had chucked up the job because his wife didn't like being left alone for a week at a time. Andre's wife didn't like it either, and soon left him. Later Crypto Corp sent him on a sales training course, which he passed with flying colours, and then transferred him to a large mining area where they had a commanding share of the market to protect.

Again he did well and was promoted to district supervisor, holding the position for some years before being moved into the branch office as branch sales manager. After more courses in management he was moved to head office as sales manager with overall responsibility for the company's sales policy.

His boss was the marketing director, an ineffective, long-service employee who spent more time on company politics than on its business. However, he took an immediate liking to Andre who was prepared to do most of the work in his department without threatening his position. He arranged for Andre to spend time overseas to widen his knowledge of Crypto Corp's operations.

Five years later the marketing director was approaching retirement and recommended to the board that Andre succeed him. The MD had suffered too long from the inefficiency of the marketing director (whom he himself had promoted into the position) and, influenced by the chairman, decided that the opportunity should be taken to bring some new blood on to the board. After a careful search they appointed a man who had held a similar position in a smaller company.

Andre was deeply shocked that he was not even considered for the position and spent much time going back over all the hardships he had endured to fit himself for it. At this rate it would take him another 20 years to get to the MD's chair. He felt he couldn't wait any longer and resigned to become the MD of a smaller company, where his years of marketing and sales experience and overseas training enabled him to turn the operation into a very profitable concern.

His departure prompted the resignations of several other promising juniors who felt, like him, that prospects were poor at Crypto.

Whether the MD's decision to bring in an outsider rather than promote from within the company was a good or bad one is almost impossible for us to judge without further knowledge of the situation. Certainly a good deal of money had been invested in training Andre and, presumably, his subordinates who left with him. Their departure meant that this potential had been thrown away and some harm had been done to morale in the organisation. However, if the selection of the replacement had been carefully made then, good as Andre might have been, the replacement must have been better and worth all the cost and disruption involved. It's always a difficult decision to make, and demands careful study and evaluation of all the pros and cons.

When a company has problems it is always an attractive thought that an outsider can be found who will bring in new knowledge and perspectives with which to create novel ways of solving the problems without being tied to the company's traditional approach.

On the other hand, unless staff can see definite prospects of promotion opening up they can become demotivated and start looking around for more rewarding jobs. This is particularly true in the vital area of 'middle management', where the experience and skills of the people in these positions often form the solid core of company performance and where promotional opportunities are invariably restricted.

There are other advantages to promoting from within. The appointee knows the company and its people so usually requires less time to settle in and become productive. Also, his strengths and weaknesses are known and can be fully utilised or addressed, whereas it may take some time (and may be costly) to find these in a newcomer.

Today good staff are expensive and hard to come by, so unless there are special reasons for hiring from outside (because of technical skills, for example) it is desirable that a thorough search is made within the organisation before looking elsewhere. Perhaps the best way to tackle the problem is to use the selection procedure we have outlined for all those thought to be eligible—inside or out—and thus ensure that only the person who best fits the criteria is chosen.

If the selection still works out in favour of an outsider it is essential that the reason for the decision is made known and frankly discussed with those within the company who are likely to be disappointed. During the discussion the 'insider' should be told honestly why he was unsuccessful, and every effort should be made to restore his self-confidence and esteem, which will have taken a beating. If possible he should be told of other opportunities likely to arise for which he will be considered, and advised of any special training he should undergo or experience he should acquire to fit himself for them. Beware of making false promises merely to placate a disgruntled employee!

Managing a merger

Following a merger or acquisition you may be faced with the need to select between candidates from two or more of the companies involved who all believe they have preferential rights to any positions going. Such decisions can be even more difficult than those we have discussed so far.

Universal and Hi-Tech had long been competitors in the computer software market. Their ongoing struggle for business supremacy had been fierce and often none too ethical. As a result each management team heartily disliked the other and this attitude extended throughout the respective companies.

Generally speaking, management at Universal tended to be more professional. The MD had a MBA degree and at least two of his departments were headed up by similarly qualified people, whilst the marketing manager held the diploma of a marketing institute. Their reputation in the market was one of reliability rather than advanced technology.

High-Tech, on the other hand, as its name implied, had been founded by a couple of computer boffins who had gathered kindred spirits over the years. Their decisions were very much made by consensus and consequently were often delayed and not always particularly businesslike.

Observing the market's trend towards larger integrated suppliers, the MD of Universal negotiated for his company to be bought out by a major equipment supplier, which gave them the necessary financial backing needed for expansion. As the purchaser already held a share in Hi-Tech it seemed natural that it should move to take them over as well, and merge them with Universal. This was duly accomplished and the day dawned when the two antagonists found themselves working for the same company.

The MD of the former Universal was appointed CEO of the new 'Universal/Hi-Tech' – a move which precipitated the immediate resignation of his erstwhile opposite number at Hi-Tech. The new CEO recognised the danger of alienating any more of the technically skilled Hi-Tech staff, but at the same time was strongly influenced by the proven competence of his own management team and his ingrained distrust of Hi-Tech personnel.

How could he maintain his standards of management and yet harness the much-needed technical skills of his erstwhile competitor, knowing that if he didn't they would be snapped up by his current competitors? It was quite a problem.

Mergers and take-overs are becoming more common these days, and selection decisions arising from these are fraught with difficulty and potential problems which can affect the outcome of the merger. However, some of the more successful predators who have addressed these problems attribute at least a part of their success to their ability to harness the often untapped management resources of their victims.

This doesn't happen by chance but is the result of a carefully planned approach by a selection team which moves in and assesses the potential almost before the ink is dry on the take-over documents.

Their approach follows the same procedure that we have outlined for other staff selection decisions, but an interesting departure is that, unfettered by custom or tradition, they have the ability to extend their search to lower levels of staff whose potential has been overlooked by the previous management. It is very often in this field that they strike gold in the form of management talents, which can make all the difference between a moderately successful and an outstandingly successful take-over.

Perhaps there's a lesson here for all of us.

POINTS TO REMEMBER

1. The potential cost of a poor decision makes staff selection one of the more important skills required of a manager.
2. The final selection must be made by the manager who will end up managing the new employee.
3. The necessary skills can be acquired by anyone prepared to take five simple steps
*   Define the job to be done
*   Develop a person specification
*   Eliminate non-starters
*   Conduct planned interviews using the 'Get ready . . . Steady . . . Go! technique
*   Decide by using selection criteria.
4. Use the same selection procedure for internal and external candidates.
5. Don't overlook the potential of lower grades of staff.

5

How am I doing?

Did you ever hear the one about the manager who said 'I thought I was doing pretty well until they fired me!'? Usually when it's told over a couple of drinks at a staff gathering it's met with nervous giggles and a quick change of subject, because it's too close to reality to be funny and it happens all the time.

At the beginning of this book we said that when employees join an organisation they are usually highly motivated but management's neglect of the basic principles of motivation gradually wears down their efforts to a bare subsistence level. If only we could maintain that initial enthusiasm and effort how much more added value would they contribute during their careers!

Earlier we explained the role of clear, achievable objectives and regular feedback of results as an important, if not the most important, element in maintaining staff motivation at a high level. Obviously if the feedback is positive—eg when an employee exceeds an objective and is congratulated on his achievement—various basic needs are met. The employee experiences recognition and a sense of achievement (both motivators) and will seek to repeat the behaviour which produced them.

On the other hand, if the feedback is negative these motivators will be absent, but the memory of them may be sufficiently strong to motivate the employee to try to do better. So a judicious mix of positive and negative feedback, such as could be expected if tight but still achievable objectives had been agreed in the first place, is likely to produce and maintain high levels of motivation.

However, if the feedback is always negative, as unfortunately so often happens, the employee will rapidly lose interest and motivation. Even worse is the case where there is no feedback at all, and the high motivation that the employees brought with them into the job is allowed slowly to evaporate over the years. It is a sad commentary on our managers that many employees hear how much their performance was valued only when the boss presents them with the department's gift at their farewell party!

An interesting research project on objectives and feedback was carried out by an American university which studied six construction sites as its sample. Having evolved a common method of evaluating performance, they set up a system of objective-setting and feedback.

Objectives were either

A   imposed externally by head office without consultation, or

B   agreed on with full participation between site and head office, or

C   not set at all.

Feedback was either

A   communicated by head office emphasising negative results only, or

B   communicated by head office emphasising positive results only, or

C   self-generated on site balancing positive and negative (results were acted upon immediately on being reported), or

D   non-existent.

A different mix of objectives and feedback was applied to each site and performance monitored over six months.

Site	Objective type	Feedback type	Performance Rating
1	A	A	5th
2	B	B	2nd
3	B	C	1st
4	C	A	4th
5	C	C	3rd
6	C	D	6th

The performance of Site 3, using participative objective-setting and self-generated feedback, was no less than 30 % higher than that of Site 6 (no objectives, no feedback). Sites 2 and 5 ran 10 % behind the leader and Site 1 shared last place with Site 6.

The research demonstrated dramatically that participative objective-setting combined with self-generated feedback were clear winners in the motivation stakes!

Monitoring and measuring results against objectives have been around since the turn of the century, when Fred Taylor and his successors first devised methods of measuring work output accurately, thus enabling the setting of realistic objectives based on observed fact. However, it wasn't until the fifties that serious attention began to be focused on other than manual workers and in areas where work output was less clear cut.

Although it was recognised that all employees up to the highest level could be motivated by a sympathetic appraisal of their performance, arriving at standards by which performance could be measured proved extremely difficult.

Early appraisal programmes called for the manager to complete a pro forma appraisal questionnaire for each of his employees annually and to forward it to the personnel office, where it could be hidden away in the employee's file until the next year. The man-

---

ANNUAL APPRAISAL REVIEW

Employee's name . . . . Position . . . .
How long in position . . . . . . .How long with company . . . . .

DIMENSION	RATING	REMARKS
Job knowledge		
Judgement		
Organising ability		
Attitude		
Dependability		
Creativity		
Interpersonal relations		
Delegation		
Accuracy		
Efficiency		

Rating:
1 = unsatisfactory; 3 = satisfactory; 5 = outstanding

OVERALL RATING IN THIS POSITION
ACTION, IF ANY, RECOMMENDED

DATE . . . .   SIGNED: . . . .

---

ager was asked to judge the employee's performance against a number of poorly defined criteria and then express his opinion of the overall performance of the subject.

Although individual managers might, over the years, have developed reasonably consistent standards in rating their own subordinates, the subjective nature of the dimensions being reviewed made it impossible for company-wide standards to be set.

However, much energy was expended in trying to make this type of appraisal more valid by specifying in great detail what the rating for each dimension entailed.

For example, accuracy would be rated on a scale running from

5 = outstanding: work is consistently accurate; mistakes very seldom made and, if made, are of a minor nature

to

1 = unsatisfactory: mistakes common and results serious; work requires regular checking and correction.

With this additional complication the completion of the form became a major operation for the manager. Because, generally, it was an unrewarding addition to their normal work, most managers begrudged the time involved and few made the attempt to complete the forms conscientiously.

The employee was often kept in the dark about his manager's view of his performance unless it was much below standard, in which case disciplinary procedures would be instituted. Thus the emphasis was mainly on negative feedback.

In the sixties 'motivation' became a popular topic, and it was realised that the appraisal could form an important link in the relationship between manager and employee only if the latter was informed of its content and allowed to comment on it. Space for this was added to the form.

```
. . .
Discussed with employee:
Signed: (Employee). . . . . . . . .Signed (Manager). . . . . . . . . . . .

Result of discussion:
```

At this point the annual appraisal became the annual nightmare for many managers. Largely untrained in interview techniques or in counselling, many were thrust into the invidious position of having to defend their highly subjective assessments to an employee who at best found the assessment difficult to accept, and at worst was actively belligerent. Small wonder that the appraisal system fell into disrepute with everyone except the dedicated personnel officer, who spent many hours trying to devise more definitive dimensions without much success. However, in spite of its shortcomings this method of appraisal is still widely used for lower-level employees.

Luckily for us all, at this time there occurred a resurgence of *management by objectives* (MBO). Although enthusiastically adopted by many organisations when first introduced in the mid-fifties, it had in the main failed to deliver on its initial promise. This was largely due to the innate resistance of managers to objectives imposed on them from above, which was MBO's original basis. However, once the system had been modified to allow full participation of employees in the objective-setting process it regained popularity and once more came to be acknowledged as one of the few management methods which ensured results.

MBO JOB DESCRIPTION			
TITLE:		NAME:	
PURPOSE:			
No	KEY RESULTS AND TASKS	STANDARDS	AUTHORITY

Job descriptions were rewritten to reflect the results the position was expected to produce and the standards by which performance would be measured. Monitoring of performance was achieved on a regular basis by reviewing results against objectives, leading to the drawing up of ACTION PLANS specifying what would be done and when.

ACTION PLAN					
Kr No	OBJECTIVE	ACTION TO BE TAKEN	BY WHOM	WHEN	
				START	FINISH

These reviews created the opportunity for normal interaction between manager and employee on work-related issues, including correcting errors and praising for work well done. Some managers believed that such interaction was sufficient and that formal appraisal was not necessary. However, the problem was that the employee never got the opportunity to assess his or her overall performance on the job or to have the boss answer the all-important question 'How am I doing?'. For this there was no substitute for the formal appraisal, and now that managers had a firm basis on which to found their appraisal discussions there was no longer any justification for not holding them.

The appraisal interview became an opportunity to look at the overall objectives of the job; to praise where they had been achieved; to enquire into the reasons for over- or underachievement; to solve problems; and to make plans for the future. Both manager and employee could look forward to the interview with pleasure instead of apprehension.

Individual applications of MBO to appraisal schemes are still being developed but generally implementation is not difficult if some simple steps are observed.

1. Start from the top

It's a commonly held fallacy that only the lower levels of employees benefit from constructive feedback on their performance and that such feedback is not necessary for senior managers who are self-motivated human dynamos, getting their satisfaction from seeing everyone else scurrying around. In fact, it is at the level of managing director and his immediate subordinates where the need for diagnosis and correction of weaknesses, and the exploitation of strengths, is greatest.

A large proportion of the organisations which succeed owes success to the leadership of top management, whilst the majority of those that fail do so because of poor-quality leadership. The immediate effect that these individuals can have on the fortunes of a company makes it essential that they are encouraged in every way towards outstanding performance. Regular appraisal by a senior qualified board member can play an important part in making this happen.

2. Review the job description

Since the appraisal is going to be based on the job description it is essential that this document is accurate and up to date. This may sound unnecessary but in practice many job descriptions, once drawn up, are left to gather dust in a bottom drawer whilst the employee settles down to fighting his daily ration of fires.

In Chapter 4 we outlined the way a job description is drawn up for a new position. The procedure is a little different for an occupied position because the incumbent should play a large part in putting it together. So the first step is to ask the employee to confirm that the KEY RESULTS (KR) listed in the job description accurately specify the primary results the position is required to achieve, and to amend the job description if necessary. They can usually be grouped under seven or eight main headings.

Then have the incumbent check that the main TASKS necessary to achieve each result are described as we showed in Chapter 4. At this stage you can review his or her efforts and add your own contribution or seal of approval as appropriate.

Next comes the most important stage of asking the incumbent to determine the STANDARDS by which the achievement of each result will be measured. To be effective these must cover all aspects of the required result and be measurable in terms of quantity, quality, cost and/or time. They should all contain a time element to

ensure that they are tackled in priority order. In some cases it may
be desirable to build in 'stretch' or tolerance limits within which
performance is acceptable.

Kr No	KEY RESULTS AND TASKS	STANDARDS
1	Major accounts are contacted monthly. 1.1 Prepare itinerary weekly to include 25% major accounts 1.2 Review call reports weekly and carry forward missed calls. 1.3 Ensure all missed contacts are covered in fourth week.	Interval between customer call reports is not more that 30 days or less than 25 days

The standard suggested above effectively monitors the sales manager's performance in relation to calling on major accounts. It
measures quantity—one call—and time—25- to 30-day interval. It
does not take into account the quality of the call in terms of customer relations or the quantity of business done during the call, but
both these aspects could be written into the standard if necessary.

Requiring an employee to analyse the job step by step in this way
will greatly assist him or her to understand it as a whole, and to see
why certain results are possibly more important than others. As we
have seen in earlier chapters, employee participation in the establishment of standards is essential if they are to be motivated to
achieve them.

It remains for you to go through the standards to ensure that they
are measurable, achievable and meet your own performance requirements for the position. If they do not you will have to negotiate new mutually acceptable standards.

3. Prepare the employee
The annual or biannual appraisal interview is probably one of the
most significant events in the working life of the average employee.
It's the time when past performance is recognised, present activities

discussed and future developments planned. As such it deserves to be accorded proper status and allocated sufficient time for it to be properly carried out.

To ensure this the employee should be notified well in advance (at least a week ahead of time) and asked to conduct some form of self-appraisal in the interim. Self-appraisal can be facilitated by asking the employee to complete a pro forma questionnaire (handed out at the time of notification) and to return a copy to you before the date of the interview.

PERFORMANCE REVIEW
SELF-APPRAISAL

NAME

1. In which key result areas do you feel you have made most progress? Why?

2. In which key result areas do you feel you have made least progress? What difficulties have you encountered?

3. What action plans should be made to help you achieve further progress — (a) in weak areas; (b) in your career generally?

4. Are there any changes you would like made to your job description?

5. Are there any other matters you want to raise at the interview?

Signed: . . . .   Date: . . . .

If the monitoring of daily progress and feedback system is working properly the employee should be under no misapprehension as to whether progress in a particular key result area has been made or not, and will fill in the pro forma with reasonable accuracy. Genuine ignorance of shortcomings on the part of the employee indicates a breakdown in the monitoring process, which will need to be rectified urgently.

PERFORMANCE APPRAISAL

NAME   POSITION   TIME IN POSITION

1.   REVIEW OF RESULTS AGAINST STANDARDS

KR NO	KEY RESULT	RATING	REMARKS

2.   OVERALL PERFORMANCE RATING

1	2	3	4	5

JUSTIFICATION:

3.   ACTION TO BE TAKEN TO CORRECT WEAKNESSES AND
     EXPLOIT STRENGTS

KR NO	OBJECTIVE	ACTION STEPS	START	FINISH

4.   DEVELOPMENT NEEDS AND PLANS

NEED DEFINED	ACTION	BY WHOM

5.   SIGNED: . . . .   SIGNED: . . . .

DATE: . . . .
REVIEWED BY: . . . .   SIGNED: . . . .
COMMENTS

4. Prepare yourself

Having set a date for the interview you will need to allocate time for your own preparation. As you will no doubt have learned to your cost in your career so far, to enter a critical face-to-face meeting without preparation is to court disaster, and appraisal interviews can be as critical as any.

The first thing to do is to arm yourself with a copy of the appraisal form. Your organisation probably has one but, if not, or if it doesn't lend itself to the participative interview based on fact which we recommend, it may be necessary to draw up something of your own.

The important headings you will need are:

1. Review of results against standards and ratings of each result.
2. Overall rating in position under review and justification.
3. Joint action to be taken to correct weaknesses and exploit strengths.
4. Future development needs and plans.

The rating scale most commonly used is a simple one.

---

1. Consistently underachieves result.
2. Occasionally underachieves result.
3. Consistently achieves result.
4. Occasionally exceeds result.
5. Consistently exceeds result.

Next you will need a copy of the employee's job description to enable you to list the key results you will be rating, and any other performance records or statistics which may be relevant. To save time you can attach the job description to the appraisal form thus enabling you to refer to each key result by its number only.

Armed with this information you can complete the first section of the form, entering the rating and remarks against each result in pencil. Although it is important not to prejudge the result of the interview, the mere exercise of writing down your ratings and reasons helps to concentrate your thoughts and provides an essential base for your later discussions. Written in pencil, your initial ratings can easily be changed if discussion during the interview warrants such amendments.

Should such a thing as a previous appraisal form exist, it would be helpful to read the most recent one completed on the employee, noting any weaknesses disclosed and, particularly, any action planned to correct them. Remedied problems of this nature can be used as a factual basis for praise (positive reinforcement) during your interview. If, in your opinion, some problems remain they must form the subject of fact-finding discussion and action plans, and be noted accordingly on the current appraisal form.

When assessing the rating for each key result it is important to consider the employee's performance over the whole review period and not to base the assessment on recent events or memorable disasters. Similarly, it is equally important to rate each result separately and not to allow prejudices either for or against the employee's overall performance to influence the assessment of individual results. Sometimes a star performer in one field acquires a halo which tends to blind you to weaknesses in another or vice versa.

5. Conduct the interview

When conducting an appraisal interview you should bear in mind the points we covered in the section on interviewing applicants for a new job. Appraisals should never be conducted in a half-hearted slapdash manner because one is dealing here with matters which are of great importance and sensitivity to the individual.

A warm supportive atmosphere is an essential component of a successful appraisal interview and this must be established in the opening minutes. As in the employment interview it is helpful to avoid the 'desk barrier' and to conduct the interview in an informal mood.

The easiest way to begin is to start working through the employee's self-appraisal, concentrating first on those areas where he or she feels progress has been made. If you can concur with the views put forward, and even supplement them with acknowledgements of other areas that are praiseworthy, you will go a long way towards creating a positive basis for the interview from which other more difficult areas can be tackled.

Once again referring to the self-appraisal, you can now ask the employee to comment on areas where he or she recognises that performance has been below standard. Negative and destructive criticism can be avoided if the discussion is focused on the problems which cause substandard results, and a problem identification and problem-solving approach adopted. This will encourage both parties to stick to supportable facts and to stay away from personal opinions.

Where the problem is a real one it is important that the employee faces up to the role he or she must play in correcting it. It is easy to allow a clever employee to offload responsibility on to someone else or even on to you. You should be reluctant to allow yourself to be drawn into the solution unless your involvement is absolutely essential.

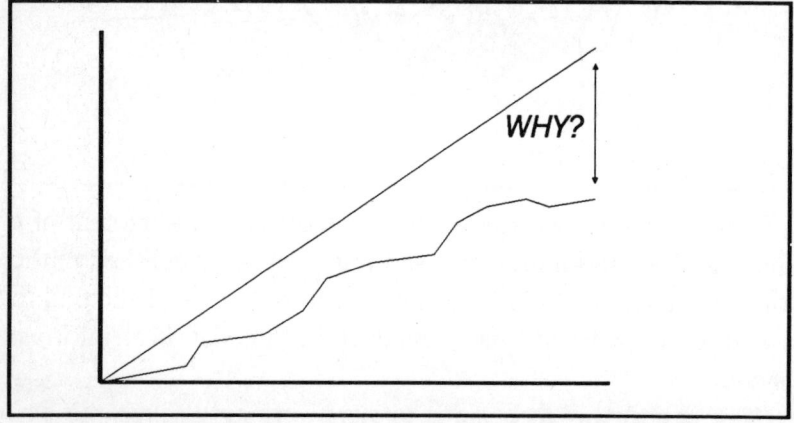

Now comes the potentially 'difficult' part of the appraisal—discussing those performance areas which have been omitted (purposefully or unwittingly) from the self-appraisal but which you have noted as being substandard. Here again, provided you stick to facts, avoid opinions (your own and anyone else's), and follow a problem identification and problem-solving approach you should not have too much difficulty.

At this stage you can complete Section 1 of the performance appraisal form, rating performance against each result and changing your pencilled figures where necessary. Hopefully you and the interviewee will have been able to agree on the accuracy of your ratings but, if not, it is still your assessment that is the final arbiter.

Major disagreement should be noted in the remarks column to guide you in future appraisals. Similarly, you can now fill in Section 2 of the form and arrive at an overall performance rating. This you should justify briefly and again, if necessary, record disagreement.

With this out of the way you can now move on to the all-important part of the interview covered by Section 3 of the form, namely the action to be taken as a result of your discussion. Here you can refer once more to the employee's self-appraisal and wherever possible accept any suggestions made therein, adding your own where appropriate.

The key to success here is clearly to state each objective before detailing the steps to be taken to achieve it. Entering the date when each task will be started and finished helps to ensure that progress is made and the objectives finally achieved.

KR NO	OBJECTIVE	ACTION STEPS	START	FINISH
1	Meet monthly calling rate	Revise schedule	1/6	5/6
		Change routing	8/6	14/6
		Increase call rate	1/7	30/7

Finally you will need to discuss any need for personal development disclosed during the interview and draw up a plan to implement the strategy jointly decided upon. This should include promotional opportunities and ways of expanding the scope of the job.

Here again it is desirable to place the onus for change and development on the employee as far as possible, because unless he or she is fully sold on the need and dedicated to doing something about it, little change will take place. Obviously if outside resources that only you can reach are required you will have to play a part in the development plan; otherwise your role should be principally one of monitoring and encouraging.

Before ending the interview briefly summarise the main points discussed, the progress made and the action to be taken, stressing the timing. Don't forget to thank the employee for his or her contribution to the success of the interview.

6. Review your own performance

When the door closes on the employee and before the ink is dry on the form, spend a little time considering your own performance at the interview by asking yourself these questions:

- Did I achieve *my* objective?
- Did I cover all the necessary points?
- Do I have the employee's commitment to action?
- Has our relationship improved?

If the answer to all these is a firm 'Yes' then you have done well indeed. However, before you get too self-congratulatory you should pass the completed form along to your own boss for his review and approval. This is particularly important when there has been some disagreement over the ratings as it helps to ensure objectivity, and avoids undue influencing of the appraisal process by personal feelings between manager and subordinate.

A well-conducted interview can be one of the most challenging tasks in a manager's job. However, it is also a very powerful management tool and can be one of the strongest motivating events in an employee's working life. As such it is well worth the effort and time taken to do it properly.

POINTS TO REMEMBER

1. Participative objective-setting and prompt feedback of results are major motivators.
2. The use of subjective appraisals of job dimensions should be limited to lower-level employees, if used at all.
3. Management by Objectives provides the basis for objective performance reviews and annual or biannual performance appraisal.
4. Six steps to a successful appraisal are:
    1. Start from the top
    2. Review the job description
    3. Prepare the employee
    4. Prepare yourself
    5. Conduct the interview
    6. Review your own performance

6

Doing it better

Apart from money, there are three major inputs into any business—manpower, materials, and machinery. Any company which purchased substandard materials or allowed its machines to operate below capacity for lack of maintenance would soon be recognised as badly managed and suffer accordingly. But any number of companies operate with untrained or poorly trained manpower, and seem oblivious to the huge loss of productivity which results.

Or at least they did, until recently. Nowadays the shortage of skills at every level, from factory floor to management suite, has become acute, representing a major restraint on present and future economic growth. Old attitudes are changing rapidly as organisations recognise that they can no longer count on picking up the

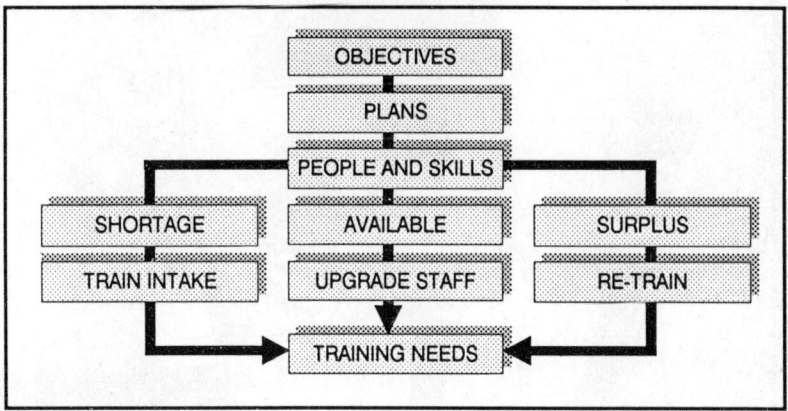

skills they need by poaching or importing them—even if they are prepared to face the high costs and disruption of their internal pay structures which such tactics usually involve. Today training is the name of the game we all have to play if we are to find the skills needed to keep our businesses alive and well and able to meet our objectives.

In business the word *training* is used very broadly to cover almost any deliberate act which encourages learning to take place. However, it can be subdivided into three main types of learning, each requiring a somewhat different approach.

EDUCATION
SKILLS TRAINING
DEVELOPMENT

Education can be defined as the assimilation of knowledge and understanding of a broad range of topics enabling the recipient to take a more active part in the economic and cultural life of the society to which he or she belongs (or aspires to). Increasingly businesses are recognising the practical benefits to be reaped by direct or indirect involvement in the education of their existing or potential labour force rather than relying on the government of the day to provide them with basic learning. Examples of bursaries, sponsorships, in-house classes and self-learning facilities are becoming increasingly common and beginning to show a modest return on the considerable investment involved.

The second type, *skills training*, is a much more specific learning of the behaviours and skills necessary to perform particular tasks to a required standard. It is usually confined to helping employees perform better in their present or intended jobs. The greater part of expenditure on training falls into this category, where the need is most obvious and the returns on the money invested are rapid and easier to measure.

The third type of training is covered by the word *development*, which we referred to in our last chapter as a by-product of the appraisal interview. It covers the provision of learning opportunities enabling an employee to develop his or her potential for advancement in a particular and agreed direction.

Although at the lower levels of an organisation these divisions are clear and well defined, as you move up the promotional ladder they become a bit blurred and less easy to measure and justify.

For example, how would you classify the training of an export manager who was learning French? Education? Skills training? Or development? And how would you assess the results apart from the risqué novels he was now able to read?

What about the managing director and his wife who visit Japan to sound out the 'culture' before taking on a new franchise? Education? Or development? Or a 'freebie' at the expense of the shareholders?

Perhaps this is one reason why training, other than factory floor skills training, has often been viewed with suspicion.

When is training justified?

Training is one activity which can greatly increase the productivity, and hence the profitability, of your business. And it can do so very quickly. However, training costs money. It takes up time which could otherwise be spent in production. It requires skilled specialists or expensive equipment or both. It takes up space. The return on investment is sometimes hard to measure. And there is always a percentage of trained people leaving for greener pastures elsewhere. To this must be added the costs of ineffective or inappropriate training where needs have been incorrectly defined or programmes poorly executed.

Most managers today realise the importance of training their staff and are keen to do so, but are often deterred by the potential problems involved. They are bombarded daily with glossy brochures advertising training and development programmes of every conceivable kind, all claiming to be the answer to every manager's problems. How does the manager decide what to do?

Well, as in any other business situation, the first step is to define the problem which has to be solved—what is actually causing the situation which is affecting the achievement of one (or more) of the business's objectives. Having arrived at the real underlying problem the next step is to consider possible solutions. If one of the possible solutions seems to be training it is necessary to answer three vital questions:

1. What needs to be done (or done better) which is not being done (properly) at present?
2. Why is it not being done already?

3. Is training the best solution?

In the first case we have to be sure that a clear discrepancy has been identified between what needs to be done to meet our objective and what is currently being done. We have to be sure that what is currently being done is insufficient to achieve our objective in terms of quantity, quality, cost or time, and that the standards we have laid down are immutable.

> To achieve a quality objective of 'zero defects' requires a high level of skill in all operators. The need to train them can be substantially reduced if we accept, say, 5 % defects as our standard. In that case the easiest solution is to alter the standards – assuming this is possible and desirable.

The second question—namely, why is not being done already—sounds elementary but there can often be more than one reason for this. When people perform poorly or act in an apparently inappropriate way it is often assumed that it is because they 'need training'. In fact there may be a whole host of reasons, including lack of motivators, presence of demotivators, failure to grasp the importance of what they are doing, other priorities, personal pressures, and so on.

Assuming that none of these is the case and that the problem is in fact an inability to perform the task to the required standard, it is still necessary to establish that training is the most cost effective solution, and that other solutions, such as reorganisation, reallocation of responsibilities, or even some mechanisation, may not be better in the long run.

Which brings us to our first rule of training which says simply:

> Training should be restricted to those problem areas where something needs to be done (or done better) by someone who presently lacks the necessary skills to do it correctly, and where there is no other more cost effective way to solve the problem.

Where do I start?

```
DETERMINE NEEDS
DETERMINE OBJECTIVES
DETERMINE METHODS
```

Determining the needs
Having decided that training is the best answer to your problem,
you next have to determine the precise training needs in the situation under review.

Training needs are defined as deficiencies in the skills, knowledge
and attitudes required by individuals in order to meet performance
criteria. So it follows that performance criteria must be defined and
present performance measured before training needs can be determined. This is usually done as part of the performance appraisal
procedure, and where this is based on clear-cut job descriptions
with measurable standards these needs are relatively easy to define.

If you don't already have job descriptions or work/task lists, or if
the problem is staffing a new operation, then it would be advisable
to draft them and determine required standards of performance before trying to determine specific training needs.

Other methods used to determine training needs include assessment centres where employees are observed whilst undertaking demanding work. This is usually confined to managers and aspiring
managers but the method has been used on other employees in specialist jobs where problem-solving and interpersonal relationships
are important. Psychometric tests, which seek to uncover less easily recognised weaknesses, are also used for specific positions. Both
these methods require the use of specialists to conduct them and
therefore tend to be restricted to larger employers.

Organisational problems—for example, excessive costs, poor-quality products, excessive scrap and waste, high staff turnover, lots of grievances and staff problems, high levels of absenteeism—are also very often pointers to a need for training. However, as we have said, these require careful analysis before being unquestionably accepted as indicating training needs.

Report from Sales Manager:
A survey of 53 sales people in the northern sales area showed that in 56 % of sales interviews they failed to close the sale due to their inability to apply an effective closing technique. In the interviews studied this represented a loss of R1 750 000 in potential sales and would suggest that a short training course on the subject would be highly rewarding.

Determining training objectives

The overall objective of the training programme should relate to one of the organisation's objectives. In the above case it may be stated as follows:

To improve the positive closing of sales interviews in the northern sales area from 44 % to the national average of 75 % by the end of the year.

Note that the objective is specific and demonstrably achievable since it is already being achieved elsewhere. Thus failure to achieve it is unlikely to be due to other causes such as product quality, price or advertising support.

In order to achieve this objective the sales people will have to learn new skills (or revise old ones) and before we can design any training for them we must decide the *learning objectives* we want to achieve. These will state the precise behaviour we expect of people completing the training.

In this case we may decide to state them as:

> Sales people completing this course will be able to:
> 1. Apply a six-step technique to close a sale.
> 2. Use a standard method to overcome objections.

Both of these are precise and can be measured to evaluate the performance of the learner *and* the training programme They also provide us with the basis for our training course and enable us to define the skills which have to be learned.

You will have noted that they do not promise that the rate of closure will improve because whether or not it does depends on many other factors which the training programme cannot influence. It would therefore be wrong to judge the training on post-course performance unless all other factors can be controlled, which brings us to the second rule of training:

> Training can only increase knowledge and skill — it cannot enforce its subsequent application.

Determining the method
Unless you happen to be an expert on everything from managing an organisation to setting up a machine, this is the point where you have to get help; and the help you will need depends on the type of training you decide is necessary. There are two broad types of training:

- On the job
- Off the job

On-the-job training, otherwise referred to as 'bird-dogging', job instruction training or (in pre-feminist times) man-to-man or sit-by-Nellie, involves a skilled worker imparting knowledge of a particular operation to a trainee actually engaged in the operation, coaching and correcting until the desired level of skill is reached. This is the most common method of training, particularly for manual skills, and has been in use since Stone Age Man made his first

axe. However, because it ties up valuable productive employees the human instructor is rapidly being replaced by the interactive video or computer programme, which takes the trainee through all the necessary steps and can endure endless failure and repetition without losing its temper or developing ulcers.

A variation of on-the-job training is the designating of a mentor or coach to whom the newly appointed employee can refer when in difficulty. Such a person is normally someone on the employee's level who can give practical advice and help without implying criticism or passing judgement, rather than a supervisor who may be inclined to both. Such arrangements are usually by their nature short term.

If individual on-the-job training is the route you intend to go you need to find someone in your organisation who knows the job or who has the skills required, and also knows how to put it across to the trainee. With his or her aid you decide the syllabus to be covered, choose the method to be used and draft an outline of the training programme, which need cover only the main headings of the activity. If the chosen method involves video or computer instruction you may need to get outside help in putting it together and there are several organisations who undertake this type of assignment.

The second type of training, and the one which supports the bulk of professional trainers, is *off-the-job training* or group instruction as it is also known. As its name implies it involves taking the trainee away from the job situation and exposing him or her to a formal training programme, usually conducted for a group of employees with similar needs, eg supervisors, managers, computer operators, etc. It can be conducted 'in house' or externally, depending on the numbers requiring training and the available facilities.

This type of training has certain advantages in that a skilled instructor or leader can impart knowledge to a number of trainees at the same time, thus making it more economical in terms of manpower and equipment. Very often a good course will develop a synergy so that participants gain more from the group exposure than they would as individuals.

But of course it does have drawbacks too. Being designed to meet the greatest needs of the greatest number, a 'standard' course may not meet the specific individual needs of trainees. Therefore it is very important to ensure that the one you select does meet as many as possible of the particular needs you have identified, by checking its learning objectives.

If you have the services of a personnel/training department they will undertake the formulation of syllabi, choose appropriate train-

TRAINING SYLLABUS		
COURSE:		
SUBJECTS	INSTRUCTION UNITS	TIME

ing methods and draft outlines for your approval. If you haven't you
will either have to do it yourself or bring in a training consultant to
help you.

A good consultant will want to conduct a training needs analysis to
ensure that the training offered will meet your needs. You can then
compare this with your own analysis, and together arrive at an outline of a training programme which will be really effective. Programmes constructed mutually in this way are likely to be far more
successful than glossy packages imported from overseas and sold
by smooth-talking salesmen with little experience of managing a
real-life work situation.

Where the number of people requiring training does not justify
an in-house programme the other option is to send the people concerned on an outside programme. Because of the wide variety of
programmes available it is again vital that you assess the suitability
of such a programme in terms of your particular needs before deciding. The easiest way to do this is to check with other users which
of their needs it met and whether yours are similar.

Information on the availability of recognised courses can be ob-
tained from:
- National Productivity Institute, who publish an annual train-
  ing directory with a comprehensive list of available courses.
- Business schools at major universities (mainly for senior ex-
  ecutives).
- Technikons in the major centres.
- Chambers of Commerce and Industry.
- Institute of Personnel Management.

Advice on the design and construction of training courses and the
compilation of schemes of work for registering courses with the Department of Manpower can be obtained from the training adviser
at your local office of the Department.

Fundamentals of an effective training programme
Whether you decide to produce your own programme or work together with a consultant you need to be aware of certain fundamental training techniques.

These are based on the need to change the behaviour of the trainee by erasing unwanted behaviour and substituting the required new behaviour. As we have seen in earlier chapters on motivation, unwanted behaviour can be erased by negative reinforcement (unpleasant consequences) and, conversely, desired behaviour can be encouraged by positive reinforcement (pleasant consequences). So the training programme must identify the unwanted behaviour and emphasise the possible unpleasant consequences of continuing it. At the same time it must introduce the desired behaviour and emphasise the rewards to be gained from it.

Before a new behaviour pattern becomes a part of life or work style it must be ingrained into the memory. Human memory can be divided into short-term and long-term components. Short-term memory images fade within hours or days. Their extinction is hastened by the superimposition of fresher or stronger images. Generally speaking, the stronger the initial impact the longer the image survives. If a short-term image is constantly reinforced the image transfers to long-term memory and becomes a part of normal behaviour.

> A lone hiker walking across a grassy field leaves a barely discernible track which disappears altogether in a few hours.
>
> However, if he returns along the same path and then repeats the journey several times a week he will within a few weeks have established a well-marked and durable path – much to the annoyance of the local farmer.

Hence there is need for a strong initial impact followed by frequent repetition for the training programme to be effective.

Memory images are created by all our senses—sight, hearing, feeling, taste and smell. Images resulting from the use of all our senses are the strongest so that actually experiencing something will produce a longer-term memory image than merely talking or hearing about it. Hence the more active involvement the trainee has in a training programme the better.

PROGRAMME GUIDELINES

1. Make learning enjoyable — provide positive reinforcement.
2. Make a strong initial impact using as many senses as appropriate — sight, sound, touch.
3. Let the trainee learn by doing as soon as possible.
4. Move from simple to complex, from known to unknown.
5. Learning is best accomplished when it follows a logical pattern.

The supporting material used in presenting a programme may take the form of mechanical aids, such as videos, films, audio tapes, slides or transparencies, or manual aids, such as a chalk board, flip-chart, etc. Printed aids may include programmed learning exercises, case studies, notes and handouts, or scripts for role-playing and workshops.

Here again, if you don't have the facilities within your oranisation there are many specialists you can call on for professional assistance. The extra cost of professionally produced material is usually well justified by its greater impact on the learners—poorly presented material tends towards negative reinforcement.

Evaluation of training

To justify the expense (direct and indirect) involved in training you must always measure its effectiveness and check that its objectives have been reached. Such measurement also allows you to improve and update the programme where necessary.

The evaluation is best divided into two parts:

(*a*) the degree to which the training objectives have been achieved (ie behaviour modified) at the completion of the course;

(*b*) improved performance on the job itself.

These should be measured separately because there may be factors in the work environment which prevent carry-over of behaviour learned on the course into the job situation. This is a major problem with off-the-job training (especially when run outside the organisation). There are literally hundreds of cases every year of good people sent away on worthwhile programmes who return filled with enthusiasm to use what they have learned only to be met with the complete indifference of their superiors, thus ensuring the extinction of their newly learned behaviour in a very short time.

In evaluating results of training it is necessary to compare performance before the training with performance after it has been given. Pre- and post-training knowledge of a subject is relatively easy to check and compare by means of verbal or written tests—

'I learned a lot — it was really helpful.'

'Good, now let's see you get back to some real work!'

the same test being applied before and after training. Analysis of the results will not only establish individual improvement but also help to identify weaknesses in the material where a majority of students answer incorrectly after training.

Where manual skills are involved pre- and post-training aptitude is also relatively easy to measure by comparison with predetermined standards—quantity, quality, time, etc. However, where non-manual skills are involved, such as selling, supervision, and interpersonal skills, measurement of post-training behaviour may be much more difficult and take much longer to assess. Here again, if the required behaviour is to achieve predetermined standards set in the job description measurement by appraisal will be factual and comparatively easy. In the absence of such standards evaluation may be vague and subjective. 'Well, it doesn't seem to have helped her much' is the sort of comment heard in such situations and causes dedicated trainers to have nervous breakdowns!

Putting it all together
The business of putting together a training programme as we have outlined it follows eight logical steps, as shown in the diagram on the following page.
However, it may not end there because, as shown in the diagram, the final evaluation may point to the need for further reinforcement or follow-up training. Generally it is advised to plan for at least one follow-up session after three to six months. This can be used to evaluate long-term retention and to reinforce learning where shown to be necessary. Thereafter future needs can be determined by a new needs analysis.

The new employee
One area where the need for training should be self-evident is in the induction of new employees. The time which elapses between an employee joining an organisation and becoming fully productive

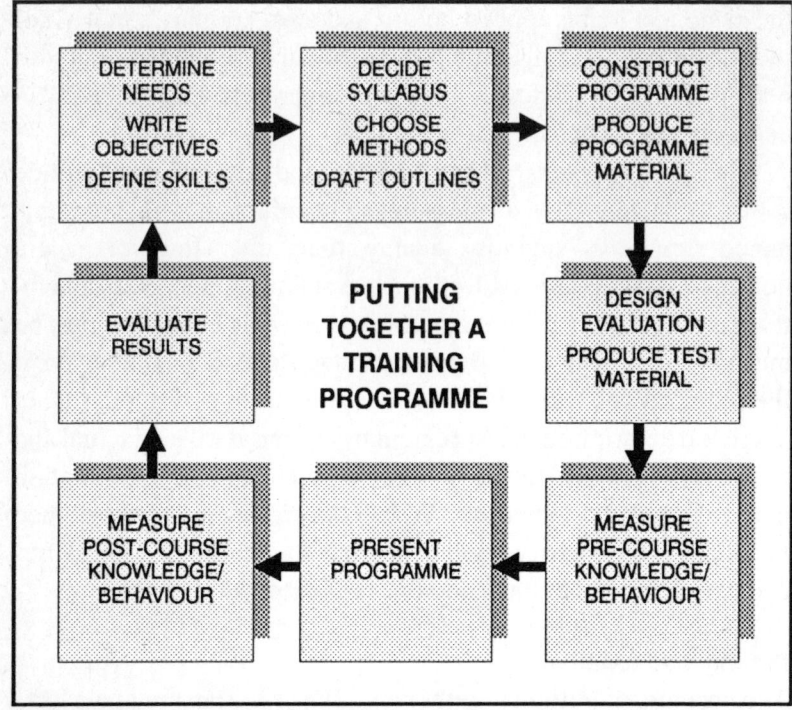

PUTTING TOGETHER A TRAINING PROGRAMME

varies with the complexity of the job, but the shorter this interval, the lower the cost of hiring the newcomer.

Imagine yourself on the first day in your first job. You know nobody; you know nothing about the organisation or its regulations and customs. You need the job and you desperately want to make a good impression, but you know you won't be able to settle down until you get to know your way around.

Meantime, almost from the first hour, you begin to pick up vibes from the other employees. What you learn from them is biased at best, incorrect and defamatory at worst, but you don't know this. You begin to form an impression of the organisation and it doesn't look as good as it did in the job advertisement. Maybe it would be better if you weren't too keen — perhaps you shouldn't try too hard until you've established yourself.

Within a couple of weeks you join the other bored, disgruntled and demotivated workers who make up 90 % of the workforce, and the organisation misses another opportunity to add a motivated worker to its human resources asset.

The message here is clear—the new employee will always receive induction training, whether provided by you or by fellow employees, and it is very much in management's interests to be first with the good news and to make a lasting impression.

Induction programmes need careful planning and need to cover three distinct areas of knowledge:

1. A general understanding of the organisation as a whole—its purpose (mission), overall objectives, activities necessary to achieve them, and its personnel practices.
2. A specific understanding of the department/section concerned.
3. A detailed understanding of the job itself and what is required of the incumbent.

Generally the first of these is covered by the personnel department or whoever does the hiring for the organisation. It can be made more effective by the use of pre-prepared audio-visual material and printed booklets to back up a formal presentation.

FORMAL INDUCTION – CHECKLIST

1. Industry background
2. Company history
3. Major products
4. Markets and competitors
5. Company organisation
6. Rules and regulations
7. Pay practices
8. Benefits
9. Employee facilities

10. Safety
11. Tour of premises
12. Employee development programmes

The second part of the induction should invariably be given by the manager concerned as only he or she can give it the necessary authority and at the same time establish an understanding with the newcomer.

DEPARTMENT/SECTION INDUCTION – CHECKLIST

1. Welcome
2. Objectives
3. Organisation
4. Personnel
5. Systems/procedures
6. Tour of department
7. Introduce mentor
8. Arrange follow-up

Most of these topics to be covered by the manager are fairly straightforward except for the last two, which may need some explanation.

Unless the manager wants to do it alone, he or she should appoint a mentor to administer Part Three of the programme and to provide a readily available source of counsel and guidance during the learning period.

JOB INSTRUCTION – CHECKLIST

1. Set performance objectives
2. Prepare programme to meet objectives
3. Put the learner at ease
4. Give instruction (one step at a time)

5. Let the learner practise
6. Follow up

Finally, it is vital that both the mentor and the manager follow up on the progress of the new employee. The frequency of such meetings on the job will vary according to the progress made, being fairly frequent to start with and tailing off as the employee gains knowledge, competence and self-confidence. If the induction programme has been successful the employee at that stage will feel an integral part of a team working for a well-run and efficient organisation.

Development training

The third type of training we outlined at the beginning of this chapter involves the development of an individual to meet the requirements of another job which usually (but not necessarily) involves promotion. This follows exactly the same cycle as any other type of training except that development objectives are determined by assessing the individual against the requirements of the new job and the training designed accordingly.

Development training can involve any of the types of training we have discussed—manual skills courses such as computer technology, external courses in management skills or particular disciplines, or simply exposure to other positions. Whatever the type of training followed it is vital that an opportunity to use the new-found skills be afforded the learner as soon as possible.

When they told Andrew he had been selected for a senior managers development course at the university business school he was delighted. Of course, it meant that he would have to work three evenings a week for the next year and give up most weekends as well, but he felt it would be worthwhile. After all, the last two managers who had been sent by the bank were now general managers at head office enjoying their new responsibilities and the salary and perks that went with them. He signed on for the course without delay.

The studying proved much more demanding than he had anticipated, but he persevered and soon was elected chairman of his syndicate, which involved him in quite a bit of extra work in presenting the cases with which they were inundated. The load meant he could spend little time with his family, and he became tired and irritable. It began to affect his marriage, his wife becoming dissatisfied with the long periods alone with their young children.

This added a new dimension to the strain under which he was living and his work at the bank began to suffer. Eventually his department was involved in a fairly serious loan default which cost the bank a good deal of money and for which he was partially blamed.

Came the day he donned an academic gown and received his dearly earned diploma, ranking fourth in his class. The same day he learned that his wife had decided to leave him. It was a considerable shock but to some degree he was borne up by his anticipation of a new job and a substantial raise.

Weeks became months and he received no word of possible promotion. Eventually he learned that a colleague from another department had been promoted to the position he had hoped for; apparently the loan debacle had weighed against him.

Two weeks later he met one of his fellow students who held a senior position in a finance house and told him they were looking for someone to fill a new high-level post. The salary and perks would considerably exceed what Andrew had hoped to get as a general manager. He applied and, with his friend's recommendation, got the job. The bank not only lost his years of experience and new-found skills but also the direct cost of his course which they had subsidised.

Manager v Personnel

In Chapter 3 we showed training as being partly a personnel function but we did also emphasise the vital role of the manager in defining needs and generally being responsible for ensuring that they are met. This division of responsibility is often not too well understood, so let's try to clarify it by quoting the final rule of training:

> It is the responsibility of all managers that their subordinates are trained to carry out their duties to agreed standards of performance. They may delegate the work of achieving this to any suitable agency, including the personnel department, but final responsibility remains theirs.

Organisations which have the resources of a well-run personnel/training department which is able to help identify needs, develop programmes and evaluate results obviously have a significant advantage. However, no matter how dedicated the specialist department may be (and they usually are very dedicated people), the overall training effort in those organisations will fail if line management do not play an active and visible role in their programmes.

So, as a manager, if your unit is not producing the profit it should, or if you want it to ensure it continues to perform well, you may need to spend some of your valuable time in considering and implementing the training route to dynamic personnel management.

POINTS TO REMEMBER
The manager's role in training should include these steps:
1. Define the problem(s) affecting achievement of the objective.
2. Decide if training is the cost-effective solution.
3. Determine training objectives.
4. Determine or approve learning objectives.
5. Produce or approve a programme to achieve them.
6. Make trainees available and brief them.
7. Ensure the results are measured.
8. Debrief trainees after training.
9. Evaluate results.
10. Follow up until the new behaviour is adopted.

7

What's it worth?

The wages you pay your staff is undoubtedly one of the key factors in your personnel policy. Remuneration affects their motivation to work and your profitability: overpayment could lead to liquidity problems and you could go broke; underpayment will result in low productivity and morale problems. It's as simple as that.

Yet, in spite of its overriding importance, in most companies the determination of wage and salary levels is haphazard and largely subjective. This is not due to any sinister intent on the part of management; it is usually a result of the way the organisation grew from small beginnings to its present size.

When organisations start up they typically recruit staff from going concerns, and tend to be obliged to offer them what they were getting at their previous employer, plus an additional amount as incentive for moving. They form the nucleus into which the new arrivals have to fit. Sometimes the new arrivals have special qualifications and are expensive. They create anomalies in the structure and after a time the anomalies outnumber the norm and the problems start to mount.

The creation and administration of an equitable remuneration structure and policy is therefore a major component of any plan to improve people management. For such a structure to be based on fact, and to be objective rather than subjective, all the jobs in the organisation must be evaluated against common criteria.

Job evaluation

The process of relating jobs to their real worth is known as *job evaluation* and is a relatively new introduction to the personnel manager's repertoire. Its main purpose is to ensure internal equity in the organisation's pay structure so that jobs at different levels are paid at the correct rate relative to one another.

Research has shown that such internal equity is a vital ingredient of industrial peace within an organisation. In fact, very often a lack of internal equity can be a greater source of employee dissatisfaction than a perceived disparity with pay levels in other organisations.

Many managers say that they have no need of job evaluation systems because they pay 'market-related' salaries. However, there are relatively few jobs where the so-called 'market' gives a clear indication of pay levels because of the wide dissimilarities between similar-sounding jobs.

Whilst it may be possible to decide pay rates for artisans and drivers, for example, on this basis, most jobs are not easily related to 'market rates'. The title 'clerk', for instance, is used to describe a very wide range of jobs at very different salary levels—the clerk of the court would hardly like to be confused with a counter clerk in an office. 'Secretary' embraces a whole range of jobs from copy typist to personal assistant to the chief executive, and even a company secretary, with a concomitant range of salaries.

Therefore, to determine equitable rates of pay for the various jobs in your organisation you must first determine their relative worth through *job evaluation*.

Introducing a job evaluation programme

A great many job evaluation systems have been developed over the years to meet special circumstances, so in the absence of the services of a personnel specialist in you organisation you may be advised to bring in a consultant to help you choose and instal the best one for your purposes. However, if you do have an in-house specialist or want to go it alone there are several points to watch before you start.

> 'I hear the old man is bringing in some consultants to introduce a job evaluation system into the company. They did that at my last place and we didn't get a rise for two years afterwards. It was a shambles. You couldn't give anyone a rise or promotion – it was all done by Personnel. They might just as well have got rid of all the middle managers. If you take my advice you better start looking for another job.'

As we have seen in previous chapters any departure from the known will induce resistance to change because it is seen as a threat to security (a basic need in us all).

So it is not surprising that the introduction of a job evaluation exercise invariably raises questions, causes some to feel threatened and initially evokes resistance from many of the staff, giving rise to the sort of 'latrinogram' quoted above. Some specific fears often heard are:

- 'It will downgrade my authority to decide on pay levels.'
- 'It is simply an attempt to reduce pay levels and introduce smaller rises in future.'
- 'This system is no good for grading particular jobs (like mine!).'

To avoid this sort of damaging situation it is essential that all the staff are briefed in advance on the exact purpose of the exercise and how it will be introduced into the organisation. This should include a full explanation of the system to be used and reassurance as to its possible effect on staff aspirations.

The probability of success is also enhanced by attention to four basic essentials:

1. To be effective, any job evaluation system must be based on written job descriptions (which, as we have already seen, are also vital for many other functions). These help to ensure that evaluation is based on the job done by the incumbent at the time, thus ensuring objectivity in grading.

2. It is advisable to involve the whole top management team in the job evaluation exercise, thus creating a sense of 'ownership' in the scheme and eliminating the bias which almost inevitably occurs if the exercise is carried out by a single individual.

3. In larger organisations management at lower levels should be involved in grading the jobs of their subordinates as they are usually more familiar with lower-level jobs than are senior management. It is, of course, a fundamental principle that nobody should be involved in grading his or her own job.

4. If your organisation is unionised you can forestall a good deal of trouble by involving union representatives in the grading of unionised jobs. Many trade unionists are not well disposed towards job evaluation systems, believing them to be loaded

against workers in favour of management. Involving them in grading and, if possible, consulting with them on the system to be used, helps greatly to gain their acceptance.

It goes without saying that those involved in the grading of jobs need to be trained in the system to be used.

Job evaluation systems

A number of systems are in use by South African organisations today. Probably the best known are the *Paterson*, *Peromnes* and *TASK* systems, and it will help your understanding of the subject if we take a brief look at their basic features.

The *Paterson* method is named after its developer Professor T T Paterson, who analysed a large number of systems during the 1950s and came to the conclusion that only one factor was necessary to differentiate between jobs, namely decision-making. He identified six different levels of decision which are common to all organisations, categorising them in bands.

- **Band F: Policy-making decisions** — made by top management to determine the scope, direction and overall goals of the total enterprise.

- **Band E: Programming decisions** — made by senior managers to formulate a strategic action plan to achieve the goals established by Band F decisions.

- **Band D: Interpretive decisions** — made by middle managers to deploy and utilise the resources needed to translate strategic plans into operational plans.

- **Band C: Process decisions** — made by skilled workers to select appropriate procedures from a repertoire of applicable procedures.

- **Band B: Operation decisions**—made by semi-skilled workers to carry out a particular operation (eg machine operators, vehicle drivers).

- **Band A: Element decisions**—minor decisions made by unskilled workers in defined tasks.

Bands B–F are each subdivided into two grades, lower and upper, indicating whether the incumbent is operating at that level (lower) or is co-ordinating others at that level .(upper). Co-ordinators of Band A workers are graded in Band B because the definition of Band A does not allow for co-ordination. These subdivisions result in eleven grades in all from A to F but may be further subdivided if necessary to accommodate particular circumstances, although this was not part of Paterson's original grading system.

The *Peromnes* system considers eight factors involved in a job and quantifies the degree of complexity of each factor in that job. Each factor has a scale of nine definitions of complexity to cover its application in all jobs from the most junior to the most senior, and each definition carries a corresponding points rating. These points are then totalled, and the job is graded using a conversion table which allocates a grade from 1++ to 19, depending on the

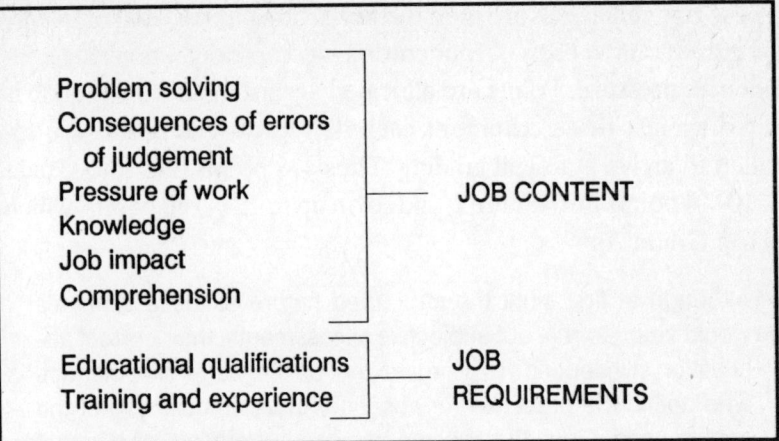

points scored. Thus a score of 2–16 points would place a very low-skilled worker in Grade 19 whilst a score of 271–288 would place the most senior executive in Grade 1++.

The *TASK* system seeks the best of both worlds by combining both the classification and points methods, first categorising jobs into five skill levels, which correspond to the Paterson Bands.

PATERSON	TASK
A Elements	I Basic (no discretion)
B Operations	II Discretionary (within routines)
C Processes	III Specialised (selecting routines)
D Interpretive	IV Tactical (managing own resources)
E Programming & F Policy	V Strategic (overall policy)

These five skill levels are then further divided into a total of twenty six grades on the basis of four criteria—complexity, knowledge, influence, pressure. Points are allocated according to how the job is rated against these criteria at each skill level. The points are totalled to arrive at a final grading. Thus 4–8 points falls into Grade 1, 10–14 points into Grade 2, and so on up to 137–140 points, which is top Grade 26.

Although at first sight the structured nature of these schemes would seem to rule out subjective assessments, their correct application still depends to a large extent on the judgement of those who define the presence (or absence) in a particular job of the criteria used. Once the scheme has been operating for a time it is relatively easy for a manager to predict the grading of a particular job and to draft the job description to meet the requirements of the grade he wants it to have.

Thus it is necessary to build into the process a fairly detailed investigation of the job by an experienced and trained third party —

which is one of the inherent advantages of bringing in a consultant to help you.

Installing job evaluation, as you can see, is a fairly complicated process and is not something to be undertaken lightly. Nevertheless, if
you have more than a handful of people working for you and are
concerned about people productivity, it is inescapable.

Pay scales

Once the task of grading jobs has been completed the next step is
to create a pay structure for the organisation. This is a matter of
deciding the mid-point and range of pay for each grade.

Desired pay ranges are normally determined after very careful
consideration of the current market rates being paid for selected
jobs in the various grades. This can be done by exchanging information with other organisations in your area or by consulting wage
surveys produced by organisations which specialise in this field.

Having obtained the data you will have to decide where you want
to be placed in the 'pay market'—ie below average, average, or
above average. To be considered 'average' you should fix the mid-
point for each grade on or around the going rate for jobs in those
grades.

Before you start to fix your new pay ranges you will find it most
useful to determine your existing ranges so that you will be able to
compare this with your desired structure and thus determine the
costs involved in implementing the new structure.

The easiest way to do this is to plot all the existing individual rates
on a graph. It is helpful to use semi-log graph paper, rather than
the conventional type, for all pay exercises because pay normally
increases exponentially through the grades; this would result in a
curve rather than a straight line on conventional graph paper. The
use of semi-log paper straightens out such curves and so makes
comparison much easier.

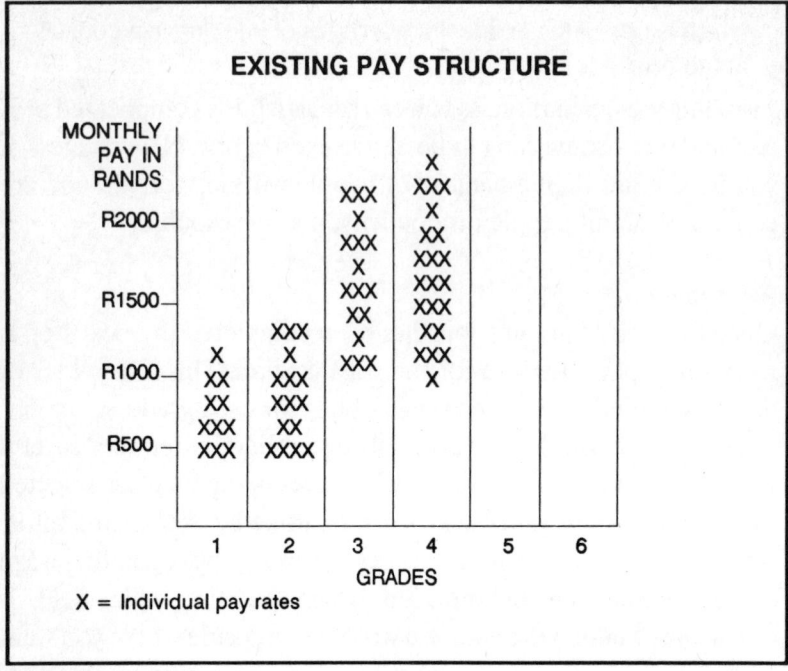

The next step is to plot the desired pay structure using the same paper. This is a matter of deciding the mid-point for each grade and the range either side of the mid-point. You will find that when a pay structure is first introduced, cost considerations tend to dictate that these are a compromise between the current situation and where the organisation wishes to set pay levels in relation to the market.

Superimposing the proposed pay structure graph on the one showing the existing situation enables you to see where the anomalies will be (ie those Xs falling outside the proposed structure) and to calculate the cost of rectifying them.

The extent of the pay range for each grade is a matter for judgement. Some overlap between grades is common, although it is advisable to limit this overlap to one grade on either side. Where existing pay ranges are already very wide it may be necessary to start

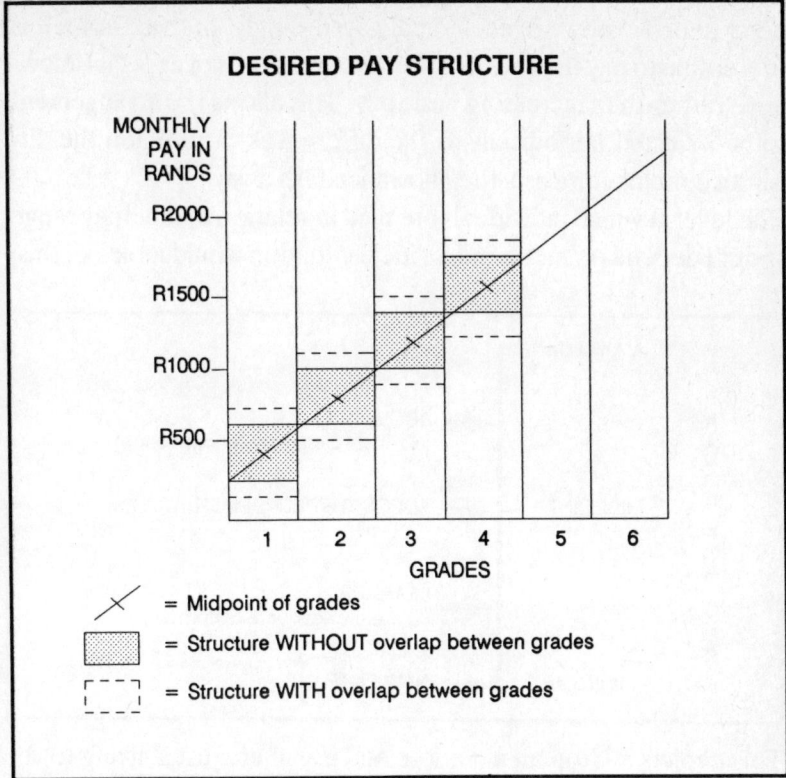

DESIRED PAY STRUCTURE

MONTHLY PAY IN RANDS

GRADES

✕ = Midpoint of grades

▨ = Structure WITHOUT overlap between grades

⌐ ¬ = Structure WITH overlap between grades

out with quite wide ranges for cost reasons and then to narrow these down over a period of time.

To do this, those below the range should be given increases to at least the minimum whilst those above should, wherever possible, be moved into more senior jobs. Where this cannot be done a common practice is to give affected employees slightly lower than normal increases over time until they are below the maximum. In extreme cases pay can be 'frozen' until it comes into line with the new pay structure.

In some jobs market shortages drive pay rates above those which would normally apply on a strict grading basis. It is unwise to upgrade jobs to accommodate this anomaly, but the situation does neėd to be acknowledged and paid accordingly. In these cases it is preferable to pay the market difference by means of a special allowance rather than increasing basic pay. This allows the arrangement to be adjusted periodically as the differences vary. When the difference no longer exists the allowance falls away.

The level at which individuals are paid in relation to their pay range should depend on merit and an ideal situation would look like this:

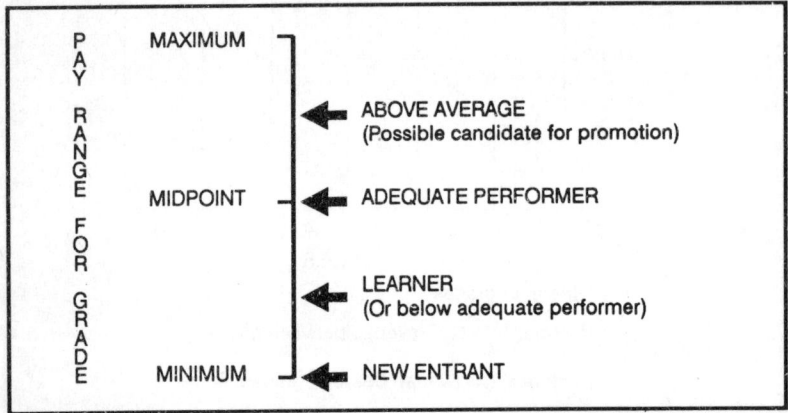

This depicts a Utopian situation, and if you are just starting to rationalise your pay structure it will probably take you some years to achieve anything like it as there will always be anomalies. However, exceptions should not be allowed to become the rule.

Remuneration packages

Pay scales normally reflect basic pay only and do not include other employee benefits—which have become increasingly important to the employee as taxation on basic pay increases. To remain competitive employers have had to offer ever more attractive benefits which include:

annual bonus	incentive bonus
medical aid	sick pay
pension/provident fund	housing subsidies

bursaries for children's education	share purchase schemes

When considering the introduction of benefit schemes you should bear in mind that employees today (particularly in unionised environments) are demanding more and more say in what benefits should be available to them and more participation in the running of the schemes. Experience shows that such consultation is highly advisable if the full 'mileage' is to be obtained from the schemes.

Many an organisation has proudly announced the introduction of a new employee benefit scheme only to learn too late that the employees concerned have little or no interest in it—usually a gut reaction to their not having been consulted.

In the UK Maggie Thatcher's well-intentioned drive to spread share ownership (and thus capitalist rather than socialist inclinations) amongst the working classes led to substantial amounts of shares being issued to the employees of some recently privatised companies, such as British Telecom, British Gas, and others.

A review of share ownership carried out twelve months later disclosed that more than 50 % of the privileged shareholders had taken advantage of rising share prices to dispose of their holdings and make a quick profit. They were more interested in the immediate gain than in having a theoretical say in the management of their companies.

At more senior levels the attraction of benefits other than pay becomes more important and, in extreme cases in recent years, so important that pay almost became a side issue! However, the introduction of taxation on fringe benefits has put an end to many of the more exotic schemes, which were in fact merely ways of avoiding or even evading tax.

Today the accent has swung to flexible remuneration packages which seek to meet the particular needs of individual executives whilst still being tax-efficient, thus reinforcing the principle of consulting the employee. For example, a bursary scheme would be of value only to an employee who has children to educate.

This is known as the 'cafeteria' approach, where an executive is told the total value of his remuneration package and is then allowed to choose how this will be made up from a range of options, each with a monetary value. Some options currently offered are:

- special housing benefits or loans
- holiday accommodation
- company cars or car allowances
- long-service awards
- special pension/medical aid payments
- share options.

The tax implications of these schemes vary and before becoming involved you would be advised to consult a reliable authority for advice.

Well, all that may seem a bit complicated and a lot of effort just to pay an employee. But if it means an employee who is not demotivated by substandard wages and who is thus available and receptive to all the motivating factors you can command it is more than worthwhile—it is mandatory.

POINTS TO REMEMBER

1. If you have more than a dozen employees you should consider introducing a job evaluation scheme.

2. Job evaluation ensures *internal equity* which is a vital ingredient of industrial peace.

3. It is essential that all staff are briefed and, if possible, consulted before introducing a system. Involvement by top management is vital to success.

4. The system must be based on written job descriptions.

5. The three best-known systems are *Paterson*, *Peromnes* and *TASK*. The last two are copyright to FSA-Contact.

6. Once jobs have been evaluated and graded pay scales can be created after first establishing the market norm for each job. This ensures 'external competitiveness'—actual pay levels are compared with those of similar jobs in the marketplace.

8

Union — friend or foe?

> 'As the Smith cannot do without his Striker, so neither can the Master do without his Workman.'

So wrote Boulton in England in 1800 to explain what was considered then as his revolutionary approach to employee relations: treating workers as responsible human beings rather than as pieces of equipment. Prior to that employee relations had been typified by the fate that befell the still-remembered Tolpuddle Martyrs, farm workers who dared to rebel against their appalling conditions and were shipped off to Australia in chains for their temerity. Even today, nearly 200 years later, some managers find it hard to change the attitudes which have shaped relations with workers over the centuries.

Werner prided himself on the way he had built up the business his father had left him, adding many new customers to the faithful core he had inherited. Many of his staff too had been with his father before him, although recently he had had to take on quite a few new workers to cope with the increasing demand. This expansion had also meant buying new machinery and he was currently suffering quite a serious shortage of cash.

Last week he was shocked to learn on his arrival at the plant that all the workers had refused to start work. When he asked the foreman what it was all about he was told that they were striking until he would discuss their grievances with the union representative.

Werner was dismayed. He knew there had been some complaints about wages recently, but surely they knew the business was going through a difficult time. He wasn't even aware they had joined a union. He felt hurt and betrayed by the people who had worked for him for such a long period and whom he regarded almost as members of his family. It must have been one of the newcomers who had stirred it all up. He would get the foreman to find out who it was and dismiss him immediately. That should bring them to their senses. See the union representative indeed – that would be the day!

That situation, with minor variations, has in the last ten years occurred hundreds of times in South Africa, where an attitude of benevolent paternalism towards the labour force has been the accepted norm. It is understandable therefore that the initial reaction to news that the workforce has joined a union is very often one of anger and hostility towards the union and its representatives. The instinctive response has often been to evict the union representatives, refuse them access, refuse to meet them, refuse to recognise that there are problems and refuse to discuss anything. And if things get really unpleasant—call in the police.

Under such circumstances it is inevitable that confrontation with the union is entrenched from the outset and relations with the workforce become soured.

The role of trade unions

The last ten years have seen huge changes take place in the field of industrial relations in South Africa. Until 1979 black workers were specifically excluded from the application of the Industrial Conciliation Act which governed many aspects of the relationship between employer and employee. Although there had been attempts to form unions among black employees, these had no legal or official status.

In 1979 for the first time black workers could organise into unions and participate in labour relations on the same basis as workers of other race groups. Like the plants which spring up when rain falls on arid land, unions emerged to represent workers in many industries. Like the plants in the veld, some were strong and healthy, others withered and were absorbed by the strong. Eventually those which survived formed umbrella bodies, the largest of which today are the Congress of South African Trade Unions (COSATU) and the National Council of Trade Unions (NACTU), both powerful organisations with considerable financial and legal resources at their disposal. Black unions have come to stay.

Despite these developments many managers, even today, still question the role of unions in worker relations and resist dealing with them. They find it difficult to understand the need for a third party in the relationship between themselves and their workers when they have managed successfully without one for so long. So let's take a brief look at the role unions have to play in a capitalist or free enterprise system.

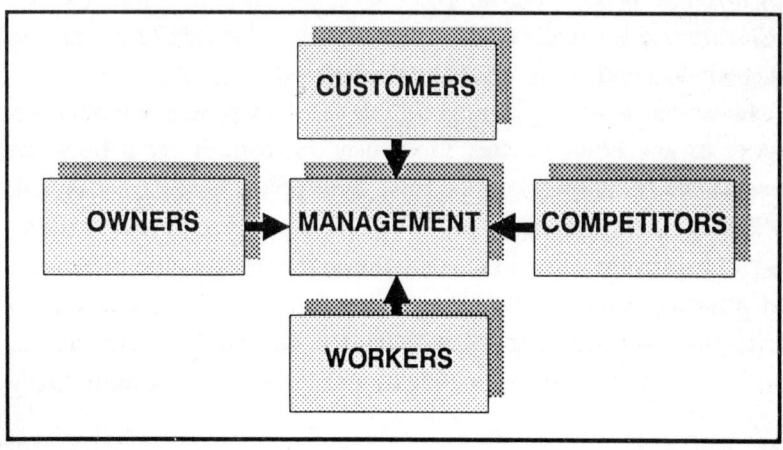

The oft-quoted model of management and workers being 'one big happy family' devoted to mutually held objectives is unfortunately wrong in many essential respects. Whilst there are many areas of common interest there are also many important areas where the interests of management and workers are fundamentally in conflict.

One of these is the area of costs and wages. Management is under constant pressure from three different quarters to keep costs as low as possible—from customers, who want better value; from competitors, who offer lower-priced products; and from owners or shareholders, who want the best possible return on their investment in the business. As we have already seen, a large proportion of these costs relate to people, directly in wages and benefits and indirectly in facilities.

Workers, in the fourth quarter, want higher wages to meet the constantly rising cost of living and of supporting their families. Expectations of better conditions and facilities are also on the increase. All these boil down to increased costs of people. This is an area of fundamental conflict between management and worker. There are others also, such as hours of work and workload.

Fundamental conflict can be dealt with in one of only two ways: by force or by negotiation. The use of force is at best a temporary solution and is usually counterproductive in the long term, leaving negotiation and compromise as the only effective alternative.

However, meaningful negotiation can only take place between more or less equal parties. Obviously this cannot occur between management and workers because their power bases are unequal, allowing management simply to dictate the course that suits them. So an important role of the trade union is to redress the imbalance of power in such situations, enabling meaningful negotiations to take place between approximate equals. The resultant agreement, although possibly less appealing to management, is far more likely to lead to a peaceful solution to the problem than the alternative of an imposed remedy.

Unions have other roles to play in industrial relations apart from confronting management in negotiations. Correctly treated, they can provide management with an invaluable source of information on the aspirations and feelings of the workforce on any of the myriad problems which beset a business today, and can materially assist in the planning and organisation of sensitive issues, such as redundancy, changes in work practices, productivity programmes and so on. It will help you to understand and work better with unions if you regard them in a positive rather than a negative light—as an opportunity rather than a threat.

Unfortunately it is as a threat that many managers regard unions. The real underlying reason why managers refuse to deal with them is that they are afraid of unions and lack confidence in their ability to deal with union representatives effectively. This confidence can only come from actual experience in negotiating—it's a 'chicken and egg' cycle.

One of the industries notorious for its poor relations between worker and management throughout the world has been the stevedoring industry, and until 1979 it was no different in South Africa.

In that year two things happened—black unions became legal and containerisation of cargo began to have a serious impact on traditional cargo handling methods, severely reducing the number of stevedore hands required. It was obvious that the labour force would progressively have to be reduced as more and more cargo was lost to the new method—but at the same time a full service had to be maintained. Strikes and other labour problems would only add to the difficulty and cost of the exercise.

Management had little previous experience of negotiating with unions and were extremely apprehensive as to the possible out-

come of the unionisation of the labour force. However, a few en-
lightened managers saw that any attempt to force through labour
reductions would inevitably lead to disruptive strikes and they pre-
vailed on the industry to deal with the new union on these matters.

It worked. Over the years the working conditions were steadily
improved but at a cost that management could justify to their ship-
owning clients. The workforce was steadily reduced from some
5 000 to less than 1 000 without major stoppages. At the same
time efficiency in terms of tons handled per hour almost doubled.

The threat was turned into an opportunity.

In most Western industrialised countries today trade unions are accepted as playing an essential role in maintaining the balance of
power between management and workforce. In many cases they
are moving into a consultative role and away from their historic ad-
versarial role. Managers in those countries have come to accept
that industrial relations is an essential and important part of the
job, demanding at least as much time and skill as the management
of their other resources. Inevitably this is also becoming the case in
South Africa where industrial relations skills are today a vital part
of an effective manager's repertoire. So let's take a look at some of
the basic industrial relations systems available to modern businesses to regulate their management/worker relationships.

Industrial relations systems
The term *industrial relations* is normally used to refer to those systems used in organisations to regulate the relationships between
groups with different and sometimes conflicting interests—usually
between management and workers.

There are four basic systems which can be used to regulate these
relationships in any organisation. These are just as necessary and
effective in a non-unionised company as in a unionised one. Indeed,

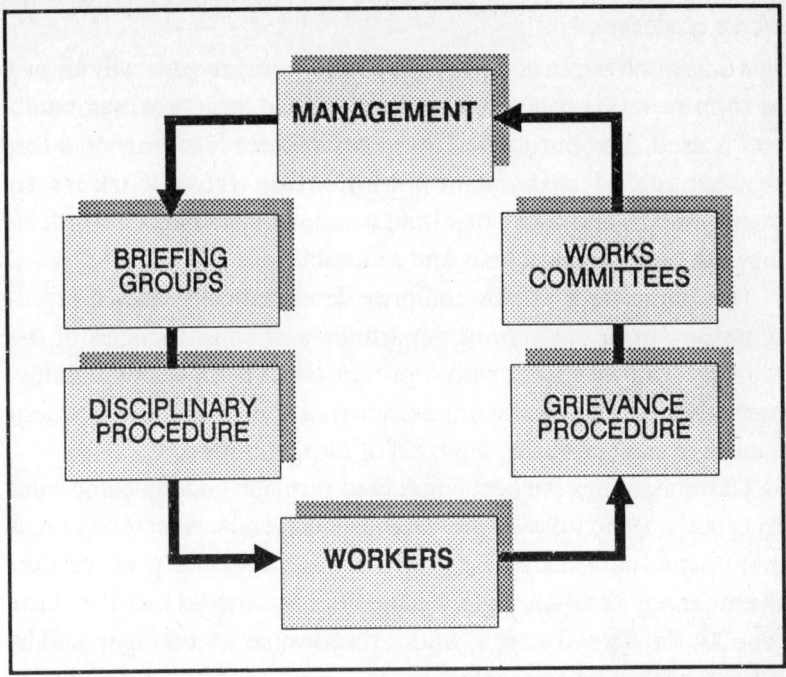

it is far better to have such systems installed and working before the union comes along than to be pushed into them after it has signed up your workers as members.

Notice that these systems complement one another—two are methods of communicating downwards and two of communicating upwards. They have two central purposes:

- to minimise conflict and maximise co-operation;
- to deal with conflict effectively when it does arise.

Unless you are particularly clued up on industrial relations and related legislation you would do well to take professional advice in the development and implementation of these systems. If you do not have the resources internally there are several consultants who specialise in this field. The Institute of Industrial Relations in Braamfontein, Johannesburg also has excellent resources in this area.

Works committees

In a unionised organisation works committees are generally known as shop stewards committees; otherwise the term 'works committee' is used. The purpose of these committees is to provide a formal means of upward communication from workers to management, and they constitute a valuable mechanism for dealing with everyday problems and requests.

The committees usually comprise democratically elected representatives from the various departments or constituencies of the organisation, who meet with representatives from senior management about once a month unless there is a reason for more frequent meetings, such as during a period of reorganisation.

These meetings are best conducted formally under a competent chairperson, and follow a pre-established agenda. A secretary takes minutes and circulates these to all members as soon as possible after the meeting. The minutes should be brief and should focus on three aspects: the agreed action; who is responsible for taking it; and by when it should be completed.

Note that these committees are a means of consultation as opposed to negotiation. Real negotiations (concerning wages, conditions, etc) can take place only with union representatives. Although shop stewards do attend negotiation meetings, the chief spokesman is usually the union representative.

Briefing groups

Whilst works committees are effective for upward communication, as we have said, they are not reliable for communicating in the reverse direction. For this purpose the appropriate system is that of briefing groups.

A committed workforce needs to be kept informed on a regular basis as to what is going on in the company in general and in their section or department specifically. This is particularly important

EFFECTIVE MEETINGS

DO:

- Ensure that action agreed is taken promptly – don't allow items to drag on over months.

- Allow and encourage worker representatives to receive proper training. It is by and large a thankless task for them and it is in the interests of both sides that representatives properly understand and execute their role.

- Have management-initiated items on the agenda as well as those raised by the workers. In this way you can use the meetings to explore problems and agree on ways of doing things better.

DON'T:

- Use the meetings as a means of downward communication to workers. Messages passed on in this manner are liable to gross distortion.

- Allow meetings to degenerate into lengthy gripe sessions – maintain time discipline and stick to the agenda.

when the company is unionised and the union communicates with its members about the company on an ongoing basis. If you don't do likewise the information your workers receive is almost certain to be one-sided and distorted.

The briefing group system starts with the chief executive preparing a written brief, which he presents to his senior executives monthly, covering the four P's:

- **PROGRESS**
  company, department, section

- **POLICY**
  changes in conditions of service, administrative procedures, etc

- **PEOPLE**
  appointments, promotions, transfers, separations

- **POINTS**
  other relevant items including agreements at works committee meetings

Each of these managers in turn briefs his own immediate subordinates, leaving out any information from the brief received which is
not relevant at their level and adding further items which are. This
process is repeated at all levels right down to the labourer.

Each manager briefs from a written document but the actual
briefing is done verbally. This is an essential feature of the system
because illiterate people can't read notice boards and the literates
often don't. Even if they do, they can't ask a notice board the questions which are necessary for full understanding.

When preparing the briefing material it is important that the information included is appropriate to the level of the employees
being briefed—there would be little point in trying to explain the
company's balance sheet to workers on the shop floor even if you
did understand it yourself! However, it is helpful to tell them how
the company is doing in general terms and particularly how their
own section is performing in terms of its objectives.

Some important points to note when setting up a briefing group
system:

- Briefs must be *brief*; not more than half an hour.
- They should be held during working hours.
- Groups should be kept as small as possible, certainly not more
  than twenty.
- People should be allowed to ask questions but not to enter into
  lengthy debates.

Disciplinary procedure
The third component of a comprehensive industrial relations system is a recognised disciplinary procedure to be applied when an
employee is in breach of company regulations.

The considerable publicity given to the large number of disciplinary cases lost by management when referred to the Industrial Court has created the impression in the minds of many managers that disciplining or dismissing an employee is no longer possible. This is very far from being the case, but it is true that many traditional standards of 'rough justice' are no longer acceptable.

Generally speaking the Court is concerned on two counts—

- that the action taken is *procedurally* fair in that it follows a fair and accepted routine
- that it is also *substantively* fair, ie that the action taken is appropriate in the circumstances that apply.

In the first case, to take disciplinary action without a formal unbiased enquiry would not be acceptable. In the second, to dismiss an employee, who has a clean record, for his first failure to report for duty on time would be deemed unfair, whereas to dismiss a persistent late-comer, who has had three formal warnings, would probably not be.

If at times it appears that the Court goes to almost unnecessary lengths to be fair to the employee at the expense of the employer, try to see it from the point of view of an unskilled worker, supporting an extended family, who may find it impossible to get another job and whose whole background and culture may be vastly different from that of the industrialised world in which he or she now has to exist.

Selina was so happy when she was able to get a job in the grading shed at Farm Industries. Although she would have to get up very early to walk to work, there was usually someone else from the village on the path and they could chat so that it wouldn't seem so far.

On her first day the supervisor showed her where to sit and told Alice, the operator next to her, to show her what to do. It wasn't difficult; all she had to do was to pick out the damaged apples and put them in a box under the sorting table for Joseph to take away when he came round every half-hour.

She had had nothing to eat since the previous day and soon began to feel very hungry. If Joseph was going to throw away the damaged apples it wouldn't matter if she ate one – or two perhaps.

The supervisor saw her take the second apple and shouted to her to come to his office. He told her she was a thief, stealing from her employers, and would be sacked that day. He took her to the pay office where they paid her a day's wages less the cost of the two apples, leaving her a few cents to take home to her mother who had sent her off so cheerfully that morning.

There was no one on the path and it took her a long time to walk home.

Although we take them for granted, our business norms and standards are often foreign to workers from rural areas and, indeed, often to town dwellers too. So it's important that there are clearly defined rules and regulations and a written code of disciplinary procedure which spells out in detail:

1. the procedures to be followed in taking disciplinary action;
2. who has the right to initiate such procedures;
3. what appeals procedure applies;
4. the types of penalty which may be imposed (usually limited to verbal warning, written warning and dismissal because of the legal complications that can be encountered in penalties such as demotion, fines, and suspension without pay);
5. the official documents to be used in recording the action taken.

Once finalised the procedure should be included in your induction programme so that it is made known to all employees from the start of their employment.

A sound disciplinary procedure is of equal value to employer and employee alike. It protects the employer against legal action for unfair disciplinary action, enabling managers to take action with confidence. At the same time each employee knows exactly what is expected of him or her and the boundaries of agreed acceptable behaviour.

Grievance procedure

The last of the four industrial relations systems, but by no means the least important, is the *grievance procedure*. Unresolved grievances tend to fester in the minds of the aggrieved like untreated wounds, spreading to others and often leading to disruptive industrial action. So it is in the interests of both management and employees to have a clear-cut effective method of dealing with

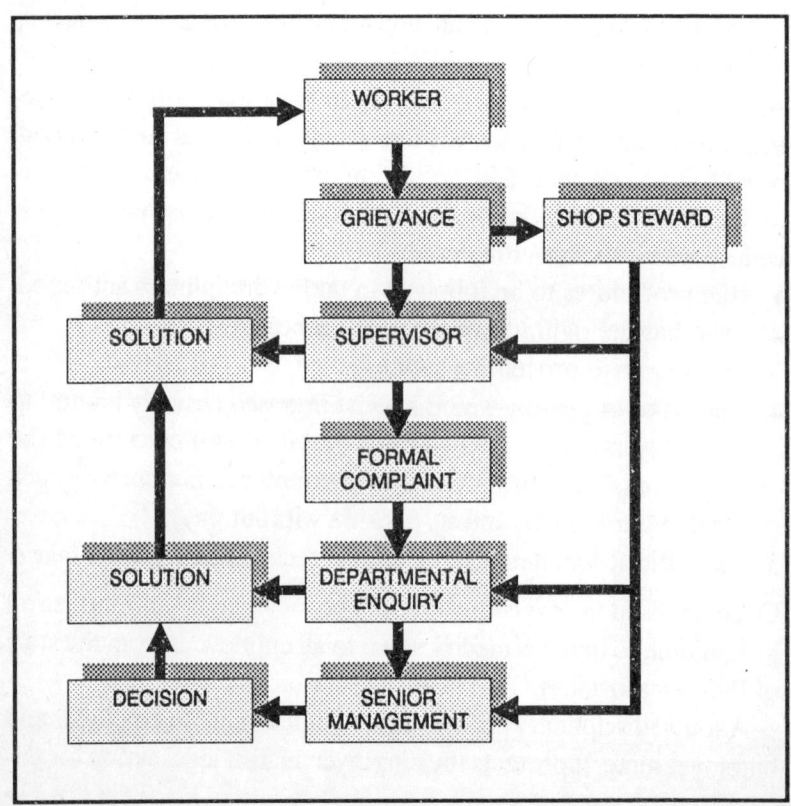

grievances as speedily and as close to their point of origin as possible.

The aggrieved worker first approaches his or her supervisor for redress. If the matter is not settled the worker refers it to the shop steward or representative, who then tries to assist the complainant to gain satisfaction from the supervisor.

If the supervisor is unable to resolve the matter it is then translated into a formal report and passed to the department manager, who convenes an enquiry to be attended by all parties concerned. Failure to resolve the matter at this level results in the proceedings being passed to senior management who must decide on the basis of the evidence before them.

Not all managers are born with the wisdom of Solomon so it is essential that those managers and supervisors likely to be involved in such situations receive proper training. It is also essential that employees are thoroughly familiarised with the procedure during their induction.

Trade unions: the initial approach

If you run a business employing more than a few workers the chances are that sooner or later you will be approached by a union representative seeking an interview. It may not be as drastic as the incident quoted at the beginning of this chapter, where the first intimation of union activity was a strike—usually it will be a simple telephonic request to see you. It would be both discourteous and unwise to refuse.

Rather it should be regarded as an opportunity to gather some essential information to guide your future actions, such as:

- How many workers does the union claim to represent? What proportion is this of the total workforce?
- Is only one interest group involved? Are other groups eligible to become members?

- Is the union registered with the Department of Manpower? If not, why not?
- Does the union have a formal written constitution? (If so, ask for a copy.)
- What are the demands at this stage? What sort of relationship is sought? Does the union want to negotiate wages, or redress certain grievances, or address other issues?
- Ask to see proof of the strength of its membership in your company, which can be done by showing you membership forms signed by your workers agreeing to pay the required subscription.

In this and in all subsequent meetings, be friendly but businesslike. It is important to keep notes on all matters discussed and agreements reached, and to confirm these by letter afterwards. At this initial meeting it is usually unwise to make commitments on behalf of your company. Rather seek an exchange of information. You can always arrange for another meeting to take matters further if necessary, once you've had time to consider all the implications.

Following this initial meeting several important decisions will probably have to be made:

- What sort of recognition am I prepared to grant the union?
- What did they ask for?
- Am I prepared to negotiate wages and other conditions of service? (Under certain circumstances you may by law have no option but to do so.)
- How will agreements reached apply to non-union members of the workforce?

There will be other matters too requiring clarification and your responsibility will weigh heavily: mistakes made at this early stage can be costly and have long-term implications. Therefore, we stress once again, if you don't have industrial relations expertise available in your company it will pay to get professional advice before you go any further.

Overview

Installing sound industrial relations procedures may not prevent your company from becoming unionised but it will certainly make the transformation a good deal easier when it happens. Installing the appropriate procedures takes time and patience because old habits die hard and racial and cultural prejudices are always in evidence, but the results, in terms of a smooth-running organisation, are infinitely worth the trouble involved.

POINTS TO REMEMBER

1. Trade unions are an accepted and recognised part of the commercial and industrial scene.
2. As such they represent *an opportunity to improve relations* between management and worker rather than a threat.
3. Industrial relations involves various systems used in an organisation to regulate relationships between management and workers.
4. *Works committees* provide a formal channel of upward communication from worker to manager.
5. *Briefing groups* provide a formal and effective communications channel from management to the workforce.
6. *Disciplinary procedures* lay down the rules to be followed when an employee is in breach of company regulations.
7. *Grievance procedures* define the method by which an employee's grievance should be handled to ensure fair and impartial treatment.
8. Initial meetings with unions requesting recognition should be regarded as opportunities to get to know each other, and decisions and negotiations should be delayed until a firm policy has been established (usually with professional help).

9

Supervision is the key

In Chapter 1 we showed in a diagram the factors which turn employees into potential profit makers. In subsequent chapters we have elaborated on many of these but so far have said little about what is probably the most powerful of them all, namely the supervision they receive on the job.

We also discussed the discretionary effort that an employee can apply to the job if so motivated.

We said that the level of minimum output is what the unmotivated employee will maintain simply to stay out of trouble. The maximum output is what he or she is capable of producing. The gap

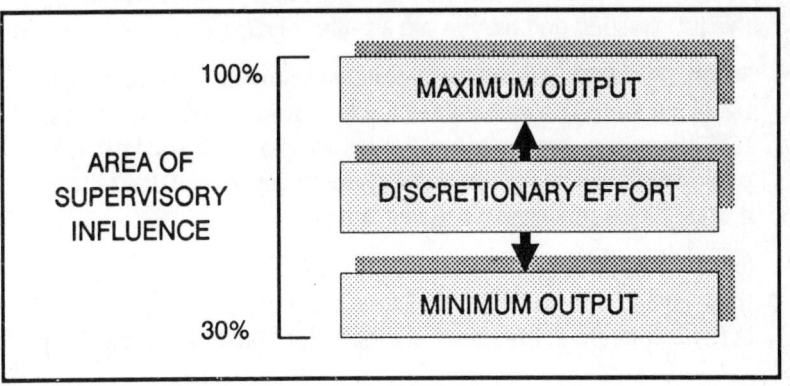

between the two is the area of supervisory influence. Thus whether the employee applies 30 per cent or 100 per cent effort depends largely on the manager or supervisor responsible for that employee.

The classic definition of the tasks of a supervisor was that he or she is responsible for planning, organising, leading and controlling the work of a section or group of employees. That definition focused mainly on production—getting the work done as quickly and as cheaply as possible—and gave little attention to the effect of those functions on the workers themselves—that was something else called motivation.

Nowadays we recognise that those four functions are in themselves the very cornerstones of motivation, and the way in which the supervisor performs them, day by day, has a much deeper significance which is not lost on the workforce.

Some of the assembly staff were taking a break while waiting for the next batch of pumps to arrive in the shop.

'Hau', said Moses, 'it's going to be one of those days when nothing goes right. Old Patchpants (the supervisor's trousers had seen better days) has started shouting at everyone. For nothing even. I wasn't doing anything and he told me he'd put me on report for loafing. It's not my fault there aren't any washers. Why doesn't he get off his backside and get some, then we could get this job finished and maybe get a better one.'

'Yeah, he started on me too', joined in Winston. 'All I did was to tell him it would be easier if we did the casings first and not wait for the washers, and he asked if I was so smart would I like to take over his job? He said then nothing would get done. I don't know. It couldn't be much worse than it is now.'

'He's the hell in because Big Eyes (the production manager wore thick-lensed spectacles) gave him a blast this morning' chipped in Esau. 'I heard it, they were standing right next to me. Big Eyes told him he could whistle for a bonus unless he improved productivity; I suppose that means some more of us will get fired now.'

'What do you lot think you're doing – holding a union meeting? Get back on the job – now!' growled the supervisor as he appeared from behind the empty stores rack.

Planning

Let's take a look first at the planning function. Most textbooks tend to play down the planning role of the supervisor, reserving it for managers and upwards. Admittedly the time scale and magnitude of a supervisor's plans may be less than a manager's but they are none the less vital to the success of the enterprise. If Patchpants's washers don't turn up on time his crew are going to be unnecessarily idle through no fault of theirs, and the labour cost element of his product will be sky-high.

But before a supervisor can plan he or she must first define the objectives to be reached. Some of these will be imposed from above but many, and certainly the detailed interpretation of even the imposed objective, have to be developed by the supervisor.

Objectives can have a substantial effect on motivation. If they are too easily attainable no one tries very hard to exceed them and many may even fail to achieve them. If they are too difficult to achieve the workers become discouraged and give up long before they have exerted their maximum discretionary effort. To be effective as motivators objectives have to hit the happy medium—

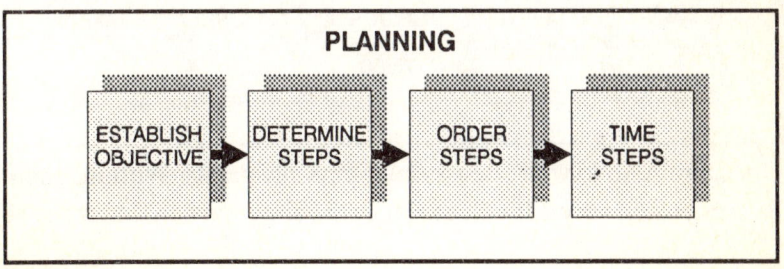

PLANNING

ESTABLISH OBJECTIVE → DETERMINE STEPS → ORDER STEPS → TIME STEPS

achievable with effort—and the best way to ensure that, unless you are a genius, is to get the workers to participate in setting them.

This doesn't require formal negotiation—simply explaining the need for the effort and asking the workers for their support is often all that is necessary for them to accept the objective and co-operate fully in its achievement.

Once the objective has been set it is necessary to determine the steps to be taken to get there, to put them in a logical sequence or order, and to decide the time needed to complete them, individually and in total. In all these activities the workers can contribute their local and particular knowledge and in doing so assume co-authorship of the plan, giving them a vested interest in its successful and timely completion.

Always remember that a poorly planned job will mean not only longer and usually harder work but will also result in strained relationships all round. So sound planning is not only necessary for maintaining production; it is a vital ingredient for good employee relations.

An essential part of planning is *problem-solving* because a problem can be defined as any situation which adversely affects the attainment of an objective, and attaining objectives is what planning is all about. A simple problem-solving sequence is as follows:

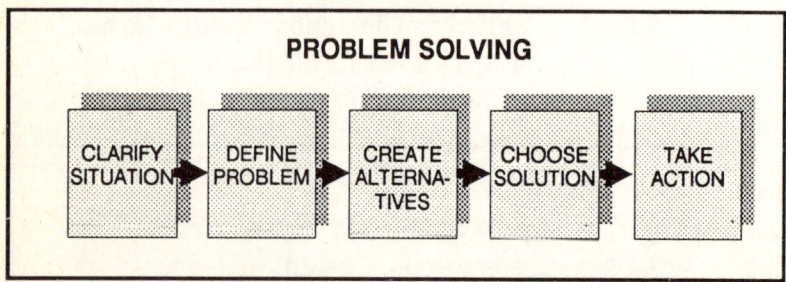

Once again, involving the workers pays dividends. Without their help it is often very difficult to clarify the situation and find the real underlying problem which is threatening attainment of the objective. Certainly workers can play a vital role in creating alternative ways of tackling the problem because of their hands-on experience. Some of the techniques which have been developed to involve workers in the problem-solving process will be discussed in more detail in Chapter 10.

Organising

We spoke earlier of the *demotivators*, those environmental conditions which discourage the worker from exerting even the minimum level of effort. By effective organising the supervisor can determine and control the presence or absence of many of these conditions.

Organising, at the supervisory level, entails obtaining, distributing and allocating the resources needed to carry out the plan (or ongoing work). As such it involves not only the people to do the job but also their tools, materials and the workplace—in fact, nearly all the elements that can create demotivators if badly organised.

SOME MAJOR DEMOTIVATORS

Incorrect team size for the job

Wrong people for the job

Wrong tools for the job

Badly maintained machinery

Poor-quality materials

Inadequate lighting/air conditioning

Badly laid out workplace

Erratic supply of materials/tools

Unfair workload

Generally, management is concerned about these factors because of their physical effect on production and they tend to overlook their even greater effect on the morale and motivation of the workers. A well-organised operation may not in itself motivate workers towards greater productivity but a poorly organised one most certainly demotivates them and thus precludes their best effort.

Whether the work environment is demotivating or supportive depends on the skill with which the supervisor carries out his work of organising. So, if you want a workforce of 'potential profit makers', one place to start is in developing the organising skills of your supervisors.

Leading
Competent organising can remove demotivators, but to introduce the motivators we have to turn to another of the basic functions of a supervisor—leading. Leading is the job of getting a team to achieve its objectives.

A team can be described as a group of people working together towards a shared objective, and the simplest example is a football team. The success of a football team will depend on three factors:

- individual skills
- motivation
- cohesion

The team manager seeks to recruit highly skilled players who are motivated to win and willing to apply maximum discretionary effort to do so. He then tries to build cohesion into his team so that individuals are prepared to work for the benefit of the team as a whole rather than for individual glory.

Similarly, to enable a supervisor to lead a team his first job is to build a team to lead.

The first step is selecting the right people and, if necessary, training them in the particular skills required. This was covered in Chapters 4 and 6.

Next comes motivation. The team's current level of motivation must be established by communicating with the members and observing them at work. Then the supervisor must try to introduce all the motivating factors we discussed in Chapter 2 to spur his team on to maximum effort, providing psychological rewards—recognition, praise, opportunities for making own decisions—where it is beyond his power to provide greater material rewards.

Finally the supervisor must strive to develop cohesion in his team so that members work happily together. The output of a cohesive team is synergistic, ie the combined output is greater than that of the same number of individuals taken together. Cohesion usually gives rise to unofficial group norms of behaviour.

'We came first in the inter-section ratings last year and we want to stay there.'
'We like to clean up around our machines every evening to make Mary's job easier.'

'We try to get it right first time.'
'We've never had to use the grievance procedure in this section —
we just talk it out with our foreman.'

'There's no point in signing on early — you don't get paid any
more.'
'Don't break your back to finish it — they'll only give you another
one to do.'
'Let the customers wait till you finish your tea — it won't hurt them.'

As you can see from these examples, cohesion can be a two-edged
sword because the norms can be either positive (and beneficial to
the organisation) or negative (and counterproductive). Positive
norms in a cohesive team result in a high standard of productivity,
but negative norms have the opposite effect and productivity suf-
fers. Teams without cohesion are not affected by either, so their
productivity does not exceed the output of their individual members.

Encouraging positive norms and discouraging negative ones are
among the most vital tasks a supervisor has to do. Luckily the same
approach will usually do both, and that is simply to apply the principles of good motivation we have discussed, and more specifically:

- Select team members who will get on together and if possible
  weed out those who do not conform and tend to disrupt the
  team.
- Communicate fully and frequently—briefing groups, appraisals, discussions, joint problem-solving all help; if they can't get
  information from you they'll get it through the grapevine,
  which is usually negative.
- Praise good team performance lavishly; when a team's achieve-
  ments are recognised its cohesion and team spirit grow.
- Encourage participation in decision-making and planning—if
  the team feels responsible it will try harder to achieve the objective; again, success will bring cohesion and positive norms.

Controlling

This is the last of the supervisory functions and is the work of setting standards, measuring results against them and determining the variances, These variances, both negative and positive, are problems which need to be solved or opportunities which need to be exploited.

Controlling is another of the supervisory functions which has traditionally been considered as being wholly concerned with the physical output of the section or team but having little to do with its motivation.

Alice was an excellent operator. All day long she sat at her bench picking up the small assemblies from the basket on her left, screwing on the end-plates, and then placing the finished assembly in the basket on her right. Alice enjoyed her work; she liked to see the pile of finished work growing and tried hard to get her basket full before the clean-up man came to take them away, bringing a new basket of incomplete assemblies.

One day a young man from the work study department came and watched her work for a whole morning. A few weeks later the works closed for the annual holidays and when Alice came back to work she found her whole workplace had been changed. Now the incomplete assemblies came down a chute in front of her and no matter how hard she worked she couldn't empty the chute — there was always another assembly waiting for her. The finished assemblies she now had to drop into a slot in her bench where they fell on to a conveyor belt and were taken off to the next section. She did not know how many she completed and no one told her.

Much to the dismay of the work study department Alice's output fell and so did that of the other workers in her section. After a month she handed in her notice, telling the foreman it was for 'domestic reasons'.

In attempting to control more effectively the work output in Alice's section, management had completely overlooked the human element. Alice was suffering from a common industrial disease—lack of feedback—which can wreak havoc with the best-laid plans for increasing control and productivity. We all need to know how we are doing, how we are progressing towards our objectives. Being able to measure progress motivates us to greater effort or gives us the much needed satisfaction that makes our jobs interesting and enjoyable. Without feedback work becomes an endless drudge and output drops.

We have already discussed the importance of employee participation in setting standards and seen its advantages in gaining their acceptance. In spite of these advantages supervisors in unionised operations are often unhappy with this approach, seeing it as an invitation to confrontation with the union which they would prefer to avoid at all costs.

Certainly, in unionised operations where standards are to be changed or new ones set, it is vital to discuss them with the workers or their representatives. As in all such cases, if the position has been properly researched and the workers have been given all the information the necessary changes can usually be effected without much difficulty.

Variances against standards are problems which have to be quantified and prevented. Here again is an opportunity to involve the workers concerned, not in a witch hunt but in a reasoned attempt to find out what went wrong and, more importantly, how a recurrence can be prevented. Such involvement increases their interest and commitment to the job, ie their motivation.

In general, supervisors approach their jobs in many different ways, some of which are helpful to building a motivated workforce and others less so. The method used depends on the supervisor's personality and training and also to some degree on the particular circumstances which apply at the time. The main styles are:

- *Directing*
  The supervisor makes the decisions and closely oversees the work. This is the traditional role of overseer, unfortunately still too common in this country.
- *Consulting*
  The supervisor encourages participation in objective-setting, planning and decision-making but reserves the final decisions to himself. This is a common role model for supervisors today.
- *Facilitating*
  The supervisor presents the team with the management objective and then leaves it to them to decide how it is to be implemented. The supervisor gives advice and assistance, and co-ordinates between teams. This is the shape of things to come and this approach is becoming increasingly common in the industrialised countries.

These three styles demonstrate the evolution of leadership over the years brought about by the changes that have taken place in the education and skills of the workforce and the increasingly technical nature of the work they have to perform. The change is radical and the key figure who has to engineer it is the supervisor who, unfortunately but understandably, often sees it as a threat to his traditional position. How to tackle the problem is something we'll deal with at length in our next chapter.

Finally, always remember that all the components of supervision—planning, organising, leading, controlling—have a very real and important role to play in changing ordinary employees into *potential profit makers* and keeping them at that level.

Which is really why we said at the beginning of this chapter that 'supervision is the key'. We need to look at it a little differently, that's all!

POINTS TO REMEMBER
1. The degree to which an employee exerts discretionary effort depends largely on the quality of the supervision.
2. The traditional supervisory functions of planning, organising, leading, and controlling (POLC) do not often affect only the material output of the unit but also have a considerable effect on its motivation.
3. Planning, which includes objective-setting and problem-solving, can benefit from worker participation in all stages, which will also help to ensure full co-operation in the ensuing activity.
4. Organising is the key function which determines the presence or absence of *demotivators* in the work environment.
5. Leading is the work the supervisor does to increase the amount of discretionary effort produced by the workers.
6. A cohesive team will produce group norms of behaviour which can be positive or negative depending on the influence of the supervisor.
7. The emphasis in leadership style is moving from *directing* and *consulting* towards *facilitating* as the workforce becomes better educated and technology increases.
8. Providing frequent feedback of results which can be compared with standards to produce variances is a major component of motivation.

10

Taking it further

So far we have been looking at some of the more traditional ways of managing personnel to achieve a harmonious and productive working relationship. We have tried to stick to methods which have been well tried and tested in practice. Nevertheless change of any sort always carries the risk of setbacks and failures which can be minimised only by careful planning. And 'change' is the name of the game in South Africa today—massive fundamental change affecting manager and worker alike.

To survive in the South Africa of the future, organisations are going to have to plan for changes which are much more far-reaching and radical than those we have covered in this book. This chapter will look at some of these changes and mention briefly some of the implications.

Unfortunately there is no general blueprint which can be used universally to guide us through this change process, and each organisation must consider what it is willing and capable of achieving in the light of its own particular circumstances.

Organisational change is never easy but it is made more difficult in South Africa by our lack of a common culture and language, and the poor levels of education generally prevalent among the labour force. These factors exacerbate racial divisions and prejudices and promote a mutual lack of trust which makes changes such as the introduction of joint decision-making extremely difficult. A real

PERCEPTION

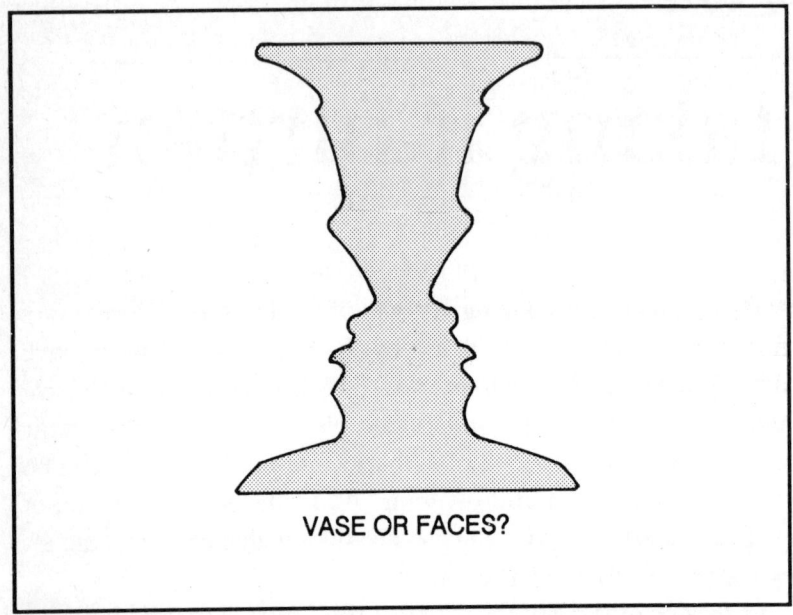

VASE OR FACES?

change in the perceptions of both parties is needed before meaningful organisational change of this sort can take place in any business situation.

Many South African managers tend to view their employees, most of whom are black., as lacking initiative, generally passive, needing constant close direction and control, with little or no ambition to improve or advance. On their part employees view managers as self-seeking racists who are more concerned with profit than with the well-being of their workforce and whose condescending attitude makes real communication impossible.

These attitudes, and the old autocratic management style that accompanies them, must be changed if we are to achieve the high levels of productivity which are necessary to survive in the economy of the future.

Two fundamental changes will be needed:
1. Organisations need to become truly multiracial at all levels.
2. There must be much greater involvement of workers in the decision-making process.

Neither of these changes can be expected to receive universal acclaim, especially in today's unsettled circumstances. However, managers genuinely concerned with productivity need to take a broader perspective and consider carefully the future socio-political environment in which their businesses will need to survive.

None but the totally blinkered can believe that our society does not have to become more integrated and better able to accommodate the rising aspirations and expectations of black people than is the case at present. If you still doubt this you have only to consider changes which have taken place in the last ten years in South Africa and project these exponentially into the future.

Not the least of the changes which managers will have to face will be in the attitudes of the workforce.

•   People will be less passive than in the past as a result of a number of factors, including better levels of education and greater exposure to the media, especially television.
•   People will be more ambitious and seek higher standards of living for themselves and their children.

These changes should be seen by managers not as threats to their traditional ways of operating but rather as opportunities to make more effective use of their human resources by involving them more in their decision-making processes. Bluntly put, the change required is to stop treating employees like children and instead treat them like adults by creating a company environment in which they can develop, grow and realise their potential whilst at the same time contributing to the growth and development of the business.

Preparing for change

An essential prerequisite to any fundamental change in management style is the existence of sound basic industrial relations systems and practices following the patterns outlined in previous chapters. There must be good two-way communication and workers must be able to expect fair and sympathetic treatment. No meaningful changes can possibly be made if the general atmosphere is hostile and confrontational.

It is also essential for top management to be visibly and genuinely committed to the need for change and be determined to make it happen. Lip service is not enough—people see through insincerity all too soon. Nearly all managers *say* publicly that people are their most valuable asset but relatively few really *act* as though they are.

People resist change because they perceive it as a threat to their security and accept it willingly only if they can see 'what's in it for them'. Change introduced without recognising this fundamental fact results in stress, opposition and reduced productivity—the very

reverse of what we are aiming for. This is why so many well-intentioned elaborate schemes introducing dramatic changes have failed, leaving their disillusioned authors to swell the ranks of the traditionalists.

So, to avoid following in their footsteps, start small. Introduce your changes in small ways, making sure that everyone knows what benefits are intended to stem from them. Let each change settle down and become routine before starting the next step. This is particularly vital when considering steps affecting productivity, which many workers instinctively distrust as being designed to increase profit at their expense.

We have already referred to studies conducted in recent years which indicate that the average worker has little or no idea as to how the business operates—where the money comes from to run it, why profit is important, what the money is used for, and many other matters we tend to take for granted. Some of the wilder misconceptions recorded were:

- the government gets the money from the people and gives it to the company
- the manager takes the money home in his (brief)case every night
- the more profit we make the more the manager gets paid (a grain of truth here probably)
- the more material we use the better it is for our brothers who make it

Such misconceptions provide a poor climate for any attempt to improve productivity.

The 6M training programme developed by the National Institute of Personnel Research (NIPR) is specifically designed to help lower-level workers understand basic business principles. Companies using the programme have reported reductions in material wastage, lower absenteeism, improved time-keeping, and many other benefits. For higher-level workers and supervisors a book, *How a Business Works* (published by Van Schaik), is available and can be used as a basis for an 'in-company' course to achieve the same results.

Working together
Having first ensured that the fundamentals referred to above are in place, managers have many further ways of tapping the hidden resources of their workforce. Perhaps the easiest and most often used is the *brainstorming* method of tackling work problems. Here a group of ten or so workers is invited to help solve a problem which is affecting the work output or the workforce.

They meet in a room set aside for the purpose where the problem is explained to them in detail. They are then asked to make suggestions which are recorded on sheets of flip-chart paper. As each sheet is filled it is hung on the wall and used by the leader to stimulate more ideas. During the brainstorming part of the session the emphasis is on generating ideas, and criticism is strictly forbidden since it has the immediate effect of turning off creative thought.

Once as many ideas as possible have been recorded the leader starts to consolidate and eliminates any which are obviously not going to contribute to a solution, leaving a short list to be considered. Those managers who regularly use this simple device confirm that it frequently uncovers ideas which would not otherwise be considered, whilst giving those attending a strong sense of belonging and participation.

Quality circles
One rapidly growing form of worker participation programme in South Africa is the quality circle. Originally imported from Japan, where education and cultural norms are very different, the system was introduced without modification in other countries; these early attempts were not entirely successful. Since then, however, it has

undergone some necessary adjustment and has been adopted by a wide range of organisations in South Africa with excellent results. There is even a National Association for Productivity and Quality Circles of South Africa which conducts regular sessions to promote the concept.

In its present form a quality circle comprises a small group of people from the same work unit who meet regularly on a voluntary basis to solve work-related problems. The members receive prior training in problem-solving techniques and their elected leaders are taught various leadership skills, such as how to conduct effective meetings. This is a vital skill as, without it, early meetings are likely to develop into gripe sessions and get bogged down in problems which should more properly be dealt with through the industrial relations channels we have described previously.

Another necessary preliminary is a thorough briefing of all those involved, including union representatives who may otherwise view the programme as an attempt by management to make bigger profits by exploiting the workers and reducing the workforce. It may help to stress that improving productivity involves working smarter, not harder, and often means easier work rather than the reverse; also that the whole concept involves moving away from autocratic management towards participation and power-sharing.

More specifically, it will be helpful to establish from the outset the precise reasons for introducing the scheme, what it hopes to achieve, and such other matters as:

- in which areas you intend to begin and why
- how success will be measured
- whether the programme will be introduced elsewhere.

Experience has shown that a 'top-down' approach generally has the greatest chance of success. This involves first training the middle and lower levels of management in the fundamentals of productivity improvement and then letting them form circles among their own subordinates. This has several advantages over a 'bottom-up' approach:

- It demonstrates management's commitment—the best way to lead is by example.
- Each level of management has to tackle productivity problems and thus knows the sort of advice and help their subordinates need.
- More senior people are usually more committed to the organisation's aims and thus more tenacious in seeking answers to problems.
- The higher the level, the greater the authority to implement the improvements and the more significant the improvements considered.

The tangible benefits arising from an enthusiastically pursued quality circle programme can make a substantial direct contribution to profits. Perhaps even more important are the indirect benefits arising from greater motivation of the workforce by participation, recognition, job interest and all the other motivators we studied in Chapter 2. All these help create the type of organisation we need if we are to tap the real potential of the workforce as discussed earlier.

Work groups

Like quality circles, work groups had been around for quite some time before anyone really took the idea seriously. Originating in Sweden in the seventies, the system was judged (rather harshly) purely on productivity results, which initially were not exciting, and the broader benefits were ignored. However, as experience was gained in the application of the programme its use spread, and today work groups are active in a very wide range of applications both in the manufacturing and service industries.

CONVENTIONAL PROCESS LAYOUT

WORK GROUP LAYOUT

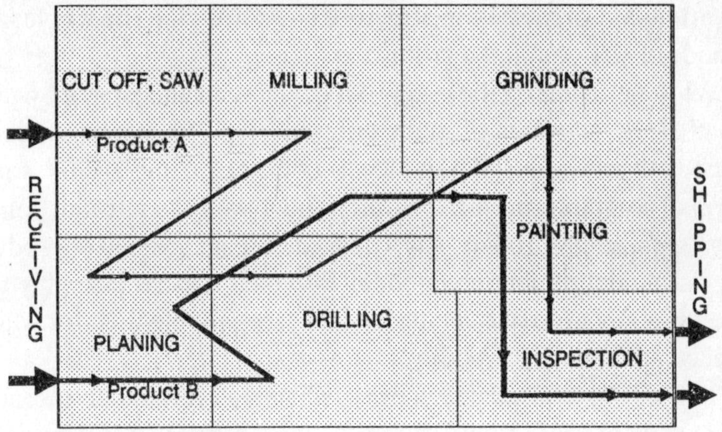

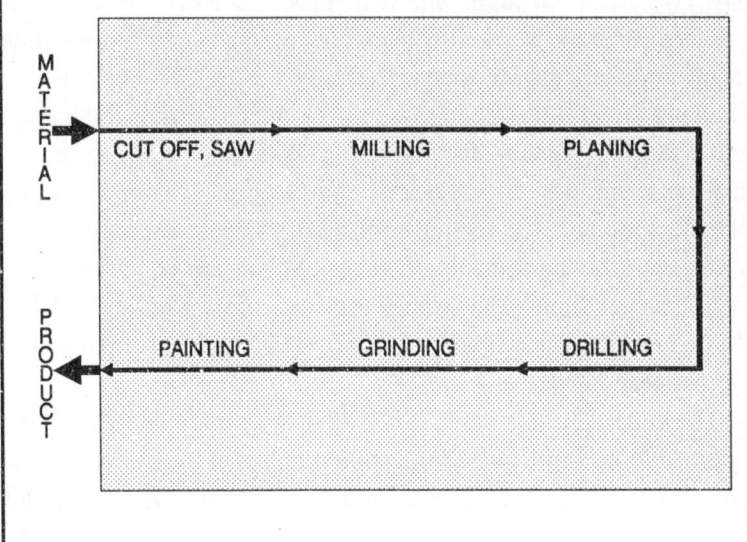

Broadly speaking, the introduction of a work group system entails breaking down the conventional manufacturing process and its attendant organisation structure and reforming the whole into a body of self-contained groups.

Whereas formerly the end product emerged almost as a by-product of the activities of many different departments or sections, each with different skills and levels of expertise and each in some form of competition with the others, now, with the introduction of *work groups*, it is produced by a dedicated team. Instead of producing an unidentifiable component for some unseen assembly the group jointly produces a tangible and recognisable item for which it accepts total responsibility.

This means that quality control, which had formed an essential and costly part of the old system, is now entrusted entirely to the group, whose members receive feedback of results directly from the end-user departments. This in turn usually results in greatly improved quality.

The same applies to loading the machines and to ordering materials, two aspects fraught with problems for supervisors and production controllers. These functions become a group responsibility, and self-imposed targets ensure that here too results improve.

Perhaps the greatest change is in the organisation of the group, which is now responsible for allocating tasks, developing skills, rotating work amongst its members, and electing its own leader or spokesperson. This means that supervisors have to exchange their traditional authoritarian role for that of an advisor or facilitator— a sort of father figure to whom the group refers when in trouble and who has the responsibility of broadly guiding the group towards its objectives.

As you can see, the changes involved in installing this method are considerable and not to be undertaken lightly. Physically relocating machinery is costly and time consuming. Training and coaching group members also takes time, as does reorienting the supervisors. It is small wonder then that initially both production and productivity may suffer, and it requires faith and dedication to live through the launch period.

However, once the wrinkles have been ironed out and people have settled down to their new and more satisfying roles, productivity and production both increase. A majority of those organisations who have tried the system speak highly of the eventual pay-off in terms of staff morale and motivation.

We have used an example from a manufacturing environment, but the technique is just as applicable to service industries, particularly where computers and high technology are involved.

The computer age is bringing with it a new generation of employees who do not take kindly to the old military-style organisations with their rigid channels of communication and precisely defined responsibilities. To obtain the best from the modern-day workforce a much looser and less formal organisation is required, and the work group can supply just that without loss of essential control.

The work group system is not yet widely used in South Africa. However, as education and expectations expand we can expect to see it becoming more popular, as has already been the case in other industrialised countries. In the mean time you could profit from some small-scale experiments along these lines against the day when you wish to introduce it on a wider scale.

POINTS TO REMEMBER

Prerequisites to major organisational change:
1. Sound basic industrial relations systems and practices.
2. Good two-way communication system.
3. A work environment free from demotivators.
4. Good managerial and supervisory skills.
5. A company culture shared by all levels.
6. Top management commitment.
7. Knowledge throughout the company of how a business operates.

New approaches
1. Quality circles.
2. Work groups.

The final balance sheet

The promise implied in the title of this book is that dynamic people management will enhance your profits. We have discussed at length some ways in which a harmonious and supportive climate may be created in which employees can develop their maximum capabilities. But what about the profit?

Let's consider the very opposite of harmony—where a bitter strike has hit a small manufacturer. The strike itself implies a large measure of dissatisfaction and unhappiness among the workforce in the period leading up to the strike. Obviously the employees would not be putting in any extra discretionary effort and so not working to their full potential. The profits would in all probability therefore be lower than the potentially achievable level for an appreciable period before the strike occurs.

During the strike itself the costs to the manufacturer are directly measurable in loss of income and cost of overheads.

After the strike there are often no winners; losses are experienced on both sides. The employees have not been paid during the strike and are under pressure from their families and creditors with the resultant stress and anxiety. Some of their colleagues might have been dismissed or might have resigned in order to seek work elsewhere. There may be even less likelihood of a harmonious motivated workforce in which employees maximise their discretionary effort, with the resultant lowering of output and profits. There are the appreciable costs of employing new staff and their subsequent training.

On the other hand, the introduction of dynamic people management will appreciably benefit both the employee and the employer. The employee is motivated, involved and challenged. The amount of discretionary effort exerted by the employee will increase. Staff turnover and its concomitant costs will lessen. Growth is inevitable.

The result of minimising friction and improving motivation is maximising profit. The choice is yours.

MANAGEMENT TITLES FROM JUTA

MARKETING MANAGEMENT — Marx & Van der Walt

Written to suit South African conditions, the style of this text is easy, while figures and tables are used liberally to explain complicated concepts. While characterised by a practical approach, the content is scientifically founded. The twenty chapters are divided into four parts. The first is a general introduction providing a broad perspective; the second deals with the marketing environment; the third with marketing decisions and the fourth part, including topics such as the product life cycle, marketing warfare, strategic marketing, product portfolio etc, deals with the integrated marketing strategy. This work is also available in Afrikaans.

WINNING WITH YOUR CUSTOMER — Anthony D Manning

Tony Manning, one of South Africa's leading management consultants and an expert in customer care, believes that obsessive attention to your customer is the surest way to boost business profits. But, he says, training "front line" people is not enough. Continuous improvement of everything is vital for success. This book helps managers to create an holistic attack strategy and the market-focused culture that it needs. It is a practical, step-by-step approach to reinventing the organisation; complete with charts, questionnaires, workshop agendas and planning guides.

COMMUNICATING FOR CHANGE — A GUIDE TO MANAGING THE FUTURE OF SOUTH AFRICAN ORGANISATIONS — Anthony D Manning

"Effective communication is a key factor in the process of productivity improvement, and this book should prove to be most useful to managers and union leaders. Its timing is most fortunate because we face the real threat that ineffective communication can do irreparable damage to labour relations and thus to our economy. This book should make a useful contribution to avoiding such a disaster."

Dr Jan Visser, *Executive Director, National Productivity Institute*

MANAGEMENT IN SOUTH AFRICA — Miller, Roome & Staude

To understand fully the vital roles and functions of management in the South African business context, this comprehensive text offers a guide to all basic and universal principles of management from a uniquely South African point of view. It fulfils a vital need for an introductory text on management.